John Webb Probyn

Correspondence relative to the budgets of various countries

John Webb Probyn

Correspondence relative to the budgets of various countries

ISBN/EAN: 9783741197406

Manufactured in Europe, USA, Canada, Australia, Japa

Cover: Foto ©knipser5 / pixelio.de

Manufactured and distributed by brebook publishing software
(www.brebook.com)

John Webb Probyn

Correspondence relative to the budgets of various countries

CORRESPONDENCE

RELATIVE TO

THE BUDGETS

OF

VARIOUS COUNTRIES.

EDITED BY

J. W. PROBYN.

CASSELL PETTER & GALPIN:

LONDON, PARIS & NEW YORK.

1877.

TABLE OF CONTENTS.

CORRESPONDENCE

BUDGETS OF VARIOUS COUNTRIES.

—◆—

INTRODUCTION.

THE public burdens of the United Kingdom have grown, during the last quarter of a century, from about 52,000,000 sterling until they have reached nearly 80,000,000. This fact has led the Committee of the Cobden Club to consider whether any means could be found to insure a more efficient control of Government expenditure. The Committee, therefore, addressed a letter to public men of various countries, in order to ascertain what controlling power was brought to bear upon the fiscal policy of their Governments. The answers which have been received are now laid before the public. They have been given by men conversant with the affairs of their respective countries, versed in economical questions, and desirous of keeping State expenditure within reasonable bounds.

The questions which the Committee addressed to its foreign correspondents were—

I. Does the Government at the commencement, or at any other stated period of the session of the Legislature, announce in detail the proposed items of expenditure for the current year? or in what other manner are such proposals of expenditure brought under the review of the Legislature?

II. Is it the practice of the members of the Legislature to discuss the proposed items of expenditure in full assembly, or are means taken, by the appointment of Committees of the Legislature, or otherwise, to investigate the proposed items of expenditure?

III. Is it the practice of the Legislature to divide the proposed expenditure into the several heads representing the principal departments of the public service? and are such divisions of expenditure referred for consideration to separate Committees?

IV. If such examination of the details of the proposed expenditure takes place by Committees appointed for such purpose, are the decisions of such Committees in regard to any reduction of expenditure subject to the revision of the Government or of the Assembly?

V. If such Committees are appointed by the Legislative body, what arrangements are made to secure their independent action?

VI. In the absence of the appointment of Committees, are any other special means adopted by the Legislature to check or control the proposals of the Government with respect to the national expenditure?

VII. Has it been found in experience that the course pursued by the Legislative body in the investigation of proposed items of expenditure, either in the military, naval, or civil services, has had the effect of keeping down the charges recommended by the Government or of limiting abuses in administration?

I am, Sir, yours faithfully,

(Signed) THOMAS BAYLEY POTTER,
Hon. Sec. of the Cobden Club.

The letters received in reply to these questions, from each country, are published in full; the method adopted in their publication being that of the alphabetical order in which the different States follow one another. This has been done with a view to facilitate reference. In almost every case the letters are preceded by a summary of the manner in which the Budget is dealt with by the Government of each country.

The reader, it is hoped, will thus have the facts of the case laid before him in such a manner as will enable him to avail himself of them with ease, and so help him to form his own judgment upon the important questions which relate to the control of public expenditure.

At the conclusion of the foreign correspondence, two articles upon it, from the London *Economist* of the 12th and 19th August, 1876, have been reprinted. They show how useful this work of the Cobden Club was deemed by so competent a judge of such matters as the late lamented Mr. Walter Bagehot.

J. W. PROBYN.

AUSTRIA.

SUMMARY.

The Austrian Minister of Finance has to lay before both Houses of the Reichsrath (Parliament) the proposed Budget of the following year, accompanied by a detailed account of ways and means.

When the Budget is brought forward, the House selects a Finance Committee of thirty-six members out of the 360 who compose the House. This Committee divides the expenditure into several heads, representing the principal branches of the public service, which are carefully examined by members specially appointed to go through the different items of the respective departments. The various proposals are voted by a majority, and the Committee presents its Budget to the House. The House has the power of accepting or rejecting the proposals of the Committee, but usually accepts them. There is no resolving of the whole House into committee as in the English parliament, but the sittings of the finance committee are open to all members of the Reichsrath. The decisions of this committee are not subject to the revision of the Government, but each minister defends and explains the budget proposals of his department before the committee.

A permanent commission for the control of the public debt, elected from members of both Houses, watches over the proposals and management of the national expenditure when the Reichsrath is not in session.

The Government lays each year before the Reichsrath an exact account of the management and disposal of the sums voted during the preceding year. This account is examined with the same care as the Budget itself.

Baron Max Von Kübeck, the writer of the following letter, testifies to the good effect produced by the parliamentary system in keeping down government expenditure and beneficially regulating the economic and financial affairs of the monarchy.

Letter from BARON MAX VON KÜBECK, MEMBER OF THE AUSTRIAN REICHSRATH.

Vienna, Sept., 1876.

SIR,—In reply to your printed circular, dated June, 1876, I first of all beg to excuse my having so long delayed the desired information, on account of two months' absence in America, from whence I only returned lately. To enter at once into the subject of the circular, and the questions therein contained, I beg to state as follows :

I. The Austrian Government, that is the Minister of Finance, must, according to the Constitution, lay every year before both Houses of the Reichsrath (Parliament) the Budget of the following year, in one of the very first sittings of the Session. He announces and accompanies its presentation with a detailed *exposé* of the expenditure, and the means of covering it, analysing the Budget in its most important items.

II. and III. As soon as the Budget is laid before the House, the latter selects a Finance Committee, composed of thirty-six members, out of the 360 who form the House. This Committee divides the expenditure into the several heads representing the principal departments of the public service, and distributes them among several Reporters. They study very carefully the different items of each respective department, and then make their proposals to the Committee, which in turn closely examines the proposals of its Reporters, voting by majority, and then presenting to the House a Budget, thus freely discussed and rendered adequate to the economical situation of the country. The House then has of course the power of accepting, rejecting, or altering the proposals of the Committee, but usually gives its assent.

It is not the custom of the Austrian Legislature, as it is of the British Parliament, to form the whole House into a Committee, as we hardly consider it possible to have a Budget of about 400,000,000 of florins of expenditure well and carefully examined by such a large body; but the sittings of the Financial Committee are public for all members, which is an exception to the rule generally observed in Austria.

It is not the custom with us to refer the divisions of the expenditure for the consideration of sub-committees, but as an exception it might be done in some cases.

IV. The decisions of the Finance Committee with regard to a reduction of the expenditure are not at all subject to the revision of the Government; but the latter, in order to co-operate in fixing the Budget with the Legislature, has to explain and defend the Government proposals, in the Committee as well as in the House; hence the minister whose department is concerned and is under discussion in a sitting of the Committee has to be present, consequently— the Committee must in the absence of a particular Minister postpone the discussion of his department till he can appear.

V. The Constitutional law of responsibility of the Ministry as a whole, and of each Minister in particular, to the Legislature; and, above all, the high-minded loyalty of our Sovereign; have always proved a sufficient guarantee and safeguard for an independent action of the Committee appointed by the legislative body.

VI. In order to control the proposals and management of the Government with respect to the national expenditure when the Committee is not sitting—viz., while the Reichsrath is not in session—there is a permanent Committee or Commission for the control of the public debt, legally appointed and elected from the members of both Houses. This Commission has to be renewed from time to time. Besides, the Government is obliged every year when the Budget is presented, to lay before the House an exact account of the preceding year touching the management and disposal of the sums allowed by the Budget legally voted within the limits thereby granted. This account is examined by the Committee quite as carefully as the Budget, and is brought before the House for the purpose of expressing either satisfaction or dissatisfaction, taking a resolution on a part or on the whole, and so indicating how errors may be avoided in the future.

VII. There is not the slightest doubt that since the adoption of full Parliamentary freedom in Austria and Hungary (about ten years ago), the greatest effect has been obtained towards keeping down the charges recommended by the Government, and limiting abuses of administration to a very considerable extent. I am proud and happy to say that perhaps few parliamentary institutions so young as the Austrian Reichsrath for the western part of the monarchy, the Hungarian Reichstag for the eastern portion, and the delegations of both Parliaments for the treatment of common affairs, such as the diplomacy, army, navy, and public debt of the Austro-Hungarian State, have worked so successfully and beneficially for the economical and financial welfare of the monarchy.

Trusting that I have fully answered the questions contained in your circular, I beg to remain,

Most faithfully yours,

(Signed)   Baron MAX KÜBECK,
Councillor of Legation, I. and R., Member of the Austrian Reichsrath, and Hon. Mem. of the C. C.

To T. B. POTTER, Esq., M.P., *Hon. Sec. of Cobden Club.*

BELGIUM.

SUMMARY.

I. The Government must lay the Budget before the Chamber of Deputies at least ten months before the commencement of the financial year, beginning in January and ending on 31st December. Thus the proposed Budget of 1877 was laid before the House on or before 1st March, 1876. This is done to give ample time for the investigation and discussion of the Government proposals.

The general Budget is divided into as many special Budgets as there are ministries.

Each minister prepares his own special Budget. The Finance Minister arranges them, and presents them to the House.

In February, 1848, a royal decree settled the form the Budget should take. The amount of the credits demanded are drawn up in detail, and are subdivided in a manner to facilitate the investigations of the Budget. Expenses relative to the "personnel" of the Government are kept apart from those relative to the "material;" thus the Government is prevented from applying moneys voted for material purposes to the increase of salaries. A more exact idea of the Ministerial acts and proposals is thus obtained.

II. Each year at the commencement of the session the House is divided into six sections. Each section examines the different budgets and names a reporter. The reporters of the various sections meet together, and form a central section or body, which nominates one of its members to draw up a Report for the House. This Report is printed and distributed in sufficient time to allow the members of the House to make themselves acquainted with it before the general debate. The general debate turns firstly on the Budget as a whole, and then each article is examined in order.

The Budgets having been voted by the Chamber are sent up to the Senate, where they are first examined and discussed by a commission of that body named for the purpose. This commission appoints one of its members to draw up a report, after which the Senate deals with the Budget as the Chamber has done.

III. As has been shown, the expenditure is divided into several heads, representing the principal departments of the public service, such divisions of expenditure being referred for examination to different committees or sections previous to the Budgets being presented to the House.

IV. Each section can propose amendments to the Budget, or the rejection of any proposal contained in it. The central section takes these matters into consideration, and if necessary consults with the Minister, and it finally decides whether or not it will advocate in the House any suggested alteration. The House, after debate, decides whether it will accept or reject any given proposal.

So, too, the Senate can amend or reject any propositions sent up by the Lower House, but no new expenditure or new source of revenue can be proposed by the Upper Chamber; such propositions can only come from the Lower House.

V. The guarantees of the independence of the sections are given by the parliamentary system. A Minister may refuse to give explanations, but he must justify his conduct before the Chamber and the Senate. The decision of the sections is merely provisional. The Government can oppose them. The Houses finally decide the matter.

VI. The law and the regulations of the House oblige the Budget to be submitted to the sections of the House; it is only in extreme cases, which rarely if ever occur, that the House can submit the examination of the Budget to a special commission nominated by the Chamber.

A Court of Accounts (*une cour des comptes*), constituted by the law of October, 1846, is charged with the examination and liquidation of the administrative accounts. It sees that no expenditure exceeds what has been passed b the Legislature, and that no transfer is made of expenditure from one head to another. It can demand all necessary information. Every senator and deputy has a right to examine all the papers of the Court of Accounts. The Court is composed of a president, six councillors, and a secretary, nominated by the Chamber for six years. Each year the Court gives an account of its operations to the two Houses, which is duly printed and distributed. No payment can be made by the Treasury without permission of the Court of Accounts. The Budget, as finally settled, is examined not by the sections but by a special commission elected at the beginning of each session.

VII. It would be difficult to find a more complete system of financial control than the one whose principal features have been summarised above. Nevertheless, the expenditure does increase, not perhaps out of proportion to the increased wealth of the country, but certainly far more than the increase of population.

Thus in 1835 the expenditure was 87,104,005 francs.
„ „ population „ 3,896,000
In 1875 the expenditure was „ 256,000,000 francs.
„ population was „ 5,336,000
In 1835 the expenditure per head was 22.35 francs.
1875 „ „ „ „ 48.00 „

When the Budget has been voted, the control of expenditure is very complete, down to the minutest details. The laws and regulations concerning the State accounts, their receipts, and disbursements, are a model of good financial arrangements which does honour to Belgium.

Letter from M. Fisco, *Directeur-Général de l'administration des Contributions directes, Douanes et Accises* (Customs and Excise), *Brussels.*

Sir,—In answer to your request I have the honour of replying to the questions you submitted to me in your letter of June 1876. I hope these explanations will be satisfactory to you. If not, I beg you will indicate the points upon which you desire more complete information.

Accept, &c.,

(Signed) FISCO.

Brussels, 15 *July,* 1876.

T. B. POTTER, ESQ. M.P.
Hon. Sec. of Cobden Club.

I. By the terms of Article 115 of the Constitution, the Budget is voted each year by the Legislative Chambers ; all expenses must be set down in it.

The Government is obliged to present the Budget to the Chamber of Deputies at least ten months before the opening of the financial year, which begins on the 1st January and ends on the 31st December. This has been done in order to give the Chambers time to judge of the demands made. It is clear that so extensive a matter as that of the Budget which embraces all branches of the Administration ought to be laid before the representatives of the nation some months before its discussion in the committees.

The general Budget is divided into as many special Budgets as there are Ministerial Departments. These Budgets consist of that belonging to the Ministry of Justice, Foreign Affairs, Home Department, Finance, War, Public Works. Each minister prepares a special Budget to meet the wants of his Department. These various Budgets are then arranged (*co-ordonnés*) by the Finance Minister, whose duty it is to present them to the Chamber of Deputies. A royal decree of 19th February, 1848, regulates, among other things, the form of the Budgets. According to this decree the Budget of each department must be accompanied by two tables : one resumes article by article the amount of credits asked for ; the other develops or draws out these articles in various sub-divisions, whose object is to enlighten the Chamber with regard to the credits asked for. Explanatory notes are added when the nature of the various public services requires it. The Budget and its explanations present the expenses for each branch of the public service. By this means the expenses relating to the " personnel " (that which regards the officials) of the Administration cannot be mixed up with the expenses relating to its material necessities; so that the Government is prevented from taking credits meant for these latter, in order to increase the salaries of the former. A clearer knowledge of the acts of Ministers is thus afforded when the financial proposals come under discussion. The Budget of each department is preceded by a note, which explains summarily, all the parts of the projected plan, and especially the increase of expenditure demanded.

II. The Budgets, and all matters connected with them, are printed and distributed among the different Committees, so that they may be discussed by them, according to the regulations of the House. Each year, at the commencement of the legislative session, the Chamber of Deputies is divided into six Committees. Each Committee examines the Budgets, and names a Reporter. These Reporters are united in a central committee by the president or one of the vice-presidents of the Chamber. The central Committee nominates one of its members to draw up a Report to the House.

The Report of the central Committee is printed and distributed in sufficient time to permit the members of the House to become acquainted with it before it comes on for discussion in the House.

The discussion in full assembly of the House, which follows on the presentation of the full Report by the central Committee, turns first upon the Budget, as a whole, and then proceeds upon each of its articles in order. Each Budget is examined and discussed by sections, and then in full house, as has been explained.

The Budgets having been voted by the Chamber of Deputies, are transmitted to the Senate, where they are first examined, and then discussed, by a commission *ad hoc* selected by the Senate from its own members.

This commission, designated Finance Commission, charges one of its members with the duty of presenting a Report to the Senate. Then follows the discussion in full Senate, as has been described with regard to the Lower House.

III. This question has already been answered.

IV., V., VI. When the discussion of the various Budgets by the Committees gives rise to proposals for reduction or increase of the estimates, these or any other proposals are examined by the central Committee, which submits whatever observations it sees fit to the Government. The Report mentions the proposals of the Committees, and the conclusion come to by the central Committee ; it makes known also the replies of the Ministers, and all are examined and discussed by the full Chamber.

Sometimes it happens that the proposals of the Committees are approved and admitted by the House, and the Budgets are altered accordingly. Sometimes the House itself reduces or increases, of its own accord, some parts of one or other Budget.

Every credit demanded which goes beyond the authorised Budget must be submitted to the same controlling powers as the Budget itself.

The 16th Article of the law touching the State accounts forbids Ministers to incur any expense beyond the credit allowed to each of them. They are not permitted to augment from any particular source the amount of credit assigned to each one of their respective services.

It is scarcely necessary to add that the Committees of the Chamber of Deputies and the Commission of the Senate enjoy the most complete independence in examining and discussing the Budget proposals.

VII. It would be difficult to establish a more severe control than that which has been set forth above in its essential features.

The answers given to the various questions raised prove that the State expenditure is submitted to a most minute examination by the Legislature, which only gives its assent when the necessity of such expenditure has been sufficiently demonstrated. It must further be remarked that an experience extending over nearly fifty years has not led to the discovery of any serious inconvenience arising from the above system of control, nor has any abuse been up to this time brought to light.

On the other hand, from the statistics published by the Government, it results that the general expenditure of the State, more especially that belonging to different services, increases each year in a proportion relatively small, and certainly inferior to the increase of the productiveness of the taxes imposed.

Letter from M. Auguste Couvreur, *Secretary of the Political Economy Society, Brussels.*

Sir,—In reply to your circular of the 28th of June I am glad to be able to give you the following information. Our law of 15th May, 1846, touching the accounts of the State (*la comptabilité de l'état*) obliges the Government to present a Budget of the public revenue and expenditure at least ten months before the opening of the fiscal year (*l'exercice*) to which that revenue and expenditure belong. The fiscal year begins on the 1st January and ends on the 31st December of the same year. The Budget account of 1877 must therefore be presented to the Chambers at the end of February, 1876. (Answer to first question.)

The Budget is discussed in all its details, like every other law, in conformity with the regulations of the Chambers. In the Chamber of Deputies it is therefore examined by the Committees sitting for the purpose. Each Committee discusses every article of the Budget, and nominates a Reporter. The Reporters of the six sections united form a central Committee, presided over by the president or one of the vice-presidents of the House. After debating the Budget, a Reporter is selected, who draws up the opinions given, and

B

the conclusions come to ; this Report is then approved and printed, after which it is discussed in full House. The discussion of the various articles of the Budget follows on the general debate.

The same proceedings take place in the Senate, with this exception, that instead of Committees permanent Commissions are nominated at the beginning of the session. There are as many Commissions as there are ministerial departments. Each Commission examines that part of the budget which belongs to it, and makes a Report accordingly.

In the Chamber of Deputies the Committees are drawn by lot each month.

The Budget discussions last several months, especially in the Lower House. The right of proposing amendments is used as in all cases, even with respect to such matters as the army estimates, which are regulated by an organic law (*une loi organique*). It is, however, very rarely that the House modifies these laws by alterations in the Budget. The previous question could be successfully opposed, should the case arise, to an amendment of this nature. (Answer to second question.)

The Budget is divided into as many parts as there are ministries. Each part is treated and promulgated like a separate law. There is no general discussion on the Budget as a whole, unless the discussion on the Budget of ways and means (the finance department) can be considered such. (Third question.)

The central Committee of the Chamber or the permanent Commission of the Senate, ask, through their Reporters, questions of the ministers, examine them, and come to resolutions, which are discussed in full house. The decisions of the central Committee and of the permanent Commission are defended by their respective members or reporters. (Fourth question.)

The guarantees assuring the independence of Committees come from Parliamentary authority. The Minister may refuse information or explanation, but under condition of justifying his course before the Chamber or the Senate.

The decisions of the Committees are only *des préavis.* The Government can oppose them. With the Chamber and Senate rest the final decision. (Fifth question.)

A Court of Accounts (*cour des comptes*), instituted by the law of October, 1846, is charged with the examination and payment of the accounts of the general administration, and of all who are accountable to the Senate. It sees that no detail of expenditure is exceeded, that there is no transfer from one head (of expenditure) to another. It collects all accounts. It can demand any information wanted relative to the receipts and outlay of state or provincial expenditure.

Every Deputy and Senator has a right to call for and examine into the papers of the Court of Accounts. The Court is composed of a President, six Councillors, and a Secretary. They are nominated for six years by the Chamber, which can at any time deprive them of their appointment, and can re-elect them. They are generally selected from the bureaux of the Court, from among the old officials of the finance department, or from among ex-Deputies. Every year the Court gives an account of its operations to the Chamber. Its Report is printed and distributed among members of both Houses.

I must not omit to state that no order for payment is discharged by the Treasury until it is authorised by the Court of Accounts.

The definite form of the Budget is made by a special Act. This Act is submitted to the Chambers in the same form and manner as the Budget. It is examined, not by committees, but by a special commission called the Finance Commission, elected at the commencement of each session. (Sixth question.)

The public expenditure and its increase depend upon other causes and necessities than their careful control. The Chambers submit to the increase, and sometimes cause it, although that is contrary to constitutional principles. But once the expenditure voted, the control is very effective, especially as against the transfer of payment from one head to another. The laws concerning the Court of Accounts, and the State management of accounts, are real models, which do honour to Belgium. (Seventh question.)

The Committee of the Cobden Club will excuse my not replying more fully, and my having delayed my reply. Absence from home, and very many engagements, are my excuses. For further details, the Belgian Constitution should be consulted, the regulations of the Senate and Chamber of Deputies, the laws touching the organisation and regulation of the Court of Accounts, the law concerning State accounts, and, lastly, a specimen Budget, with the reports belonging to it. If these documents are not to be found in the Library of the House of Commons, I could send them to the Cobden Club as a slight proof of my gratitude for the honour done me in admitting me as one of its members from its very commencement.

Accept, gentlemen, &c.,

(Signed)   Auguste Couvreur.

Letter from M. Ad. Le Hardy de Beaulieu, *Professor of Political Economy, and Member of the Belgian Parliament.*

I received this morning your circular of the 28th June, 1876, in which you ask your foreign members to tell you the means employed in Belgium and elsewhere, for criticising and controlling the expenditure of the Executive, by the votes of the Legislature, and especially of the Chamber of Deputies.

The Committee of the Cobden Club has given its serious attention to the evils which the great increase of the public expenditure has entailed on the people, and to the ineffectual efforts of Parliament to control this continual increase. The Committee is desirous of knowing whether such is the case in Belgium.

I am about to reply to your questions as briefly as possible, endeavouring to show the causes which have led, in

Belgium, to the enormous increase of our annual Budgets, in all their branches without exception, causes which, in my judgment, will long continue to operate.

In order to give you an exact idea of the progressive increase of our expenses since 1830, the date of our separation from Holland, I send the following table of expenses, beginning with the year 1835. I have begun with this year because Belgium was then fully re-organised after her revolution, and entered into a normal and regular condition.

1835.	Expenses	... ...	87,104,005 francs.
	Population	... ...	3,896,900
	Expense per head	...	22.35 francs.
1845.	Expenses	... ...	134,389,350 francs.
	Population	... ...	4,250,000
	Expense per head	...	31.62 francs.
1855.	Expenses	...	146,926,212 francs.
	Population	...	4,579,000
	Expense per head		32.08 francs.
1865	Expenses	...	188,793,736 francs.
	Population	...	4,910,000
	Expense per head		38.45 francs.
1870.	Expenses	... ...	216,907,800 francs.
	Population	... ...	5,087,800
	Expense per head	...	42.63 francs.
1875.	Expenses	... ...	256,000,000 francs.
	Population	... ...	5,336,000
	Expense per head	...	48 francs.

The expenditure has therefore tripled in forty years, although the population has hardly increased more than a third.

Having said thus much, I proceed to answer your seven questions.

I. The law of the 15th May, 1846, which organises the State accounts, obliges the Government to lay upon the table of the Chamber of Deputies (which alone has the initiative with regard to finance and the army contingent) the proposed Budget of receipts and expenditure; all the receipts and all the expenditure of the State must be set down in the Budget and in the public accounts.

Although there are only six ministerial departments, there are eleven Budgets.

a. The Budget of ways and means (*voies et moyens*), which must comprise the whole of the receipts.

b. The Finance Budget, which includes all the sums expended in the administration of the State finances.

c. The Budget of the Public Debt, which includes the interest and the redemption of the National Debt, the expenses of administration of these debts and loans; the guarantees of interest to the societies to whom concessions of public works have been given, especially railways; civil and military grants, and pensions, &c. &c. These three Budgets belong to the department of the Ministry of Finance.

d. The Budget of Justice comprises the salaries of magistrates, the general expenses of police, and of the detention of prisoners, the salaries of the ministers of different denominations.

e. The Budget of the Interior comprises, besides the central administration, that of the provinces and districts (*arrondissements*), public instruction in all its parts, arts, and literature; the cross roads; sanitary condition of towns and country districts.

f. The Budget of Foreign Affairs comprises diplomatic expenses. The Naval Budget has been recently separated from that of Foreign Affairs.

g. The War Budget comprises the army, fortifications, artillery, &c., &c.

h. The Budget of the Gendarmerie, which should logically belong to the Ministry of Justice, has recently been detached from the army, and forms a separate administration under the jurisdiction of the Minister of War.

i. The Budget of the *recettes pour ordre* comprises State receipts and expenditure *pour compte de tiers.*

k. The Budget of *non-valeurs* comprises receipts lost and annulled (*comprend les pertes et annulations de recettes*).

l. The Budget of Public Works has become the principal one, from the largeness of its amount. It is now greater than the general Budget of the kingdom was forty years ago. It comprises, besides the expenses of administration, the maintenance of roads, canals, rivers, ports, and dykes, State buildings, post-offices, telegraphs, steamboats, the construction of new lines, &c., as well as the working of the railways, post-offices, telegraphs, and steamers, &c.

All these Budgets must be made out before the 1st of March. They are printed and distributed at once, and may be examined by the Committees before the close of the session. It sometimes happens that several Budgets made out by the 1st of March are voted as early as May or June. The Budgets are divided into chapters and articles. There can be no transference of what comes under a given chapter or article to another chapter and article, unless the law approving the Budget expressly authorises.

The Court of Accounts (*la Cour de Comptes*) instituted by the law of the 29th October, 1846, whose members are nominated for six years by the Chamber of Representatives, is specially charged to take care that no sum, however small it may be, leaves the Exchequer unless its expenditure has been formally authorised by one of the articles of the Budget.

II. The Budgets, like all projects of law, with rare exceptions, are referred to the Committees of the month in which the projects have been presented. The Chamber is, in fact, divided into six Committees, drawn by lot, at the first sitting of every month. They immediately nominate their president, vice-president, secretary, and delegate to the Commission of Petitions.

The Committees are called together, nominally by their president, but really by the Bureau, sometimes on the demand of the Minister, or on that of the author of an amendment or of a proposal.

All the Committees examine all the Budgets successively and separately, article by article. The committees state, in a document drawn up by the secretary, their observations, questions, amendments, or votes.

They nominate a special Reporter for each Budget. The six Reporters of the Committees presided over by the President of the Chamber, or one of the vice-presidents, form what is called the Central Committee. This body (after making itself acquainted with the decisions come to in each one of the six Committees, and of the questions to be submitted to the central body, the Government, or the particular Minister whom it may concern), examines the proposed Budget, sees if the figures be correct, obtains from the Minister or the Government the necessary explanations, the documents which are deemed requisite, and questions the ministers either verbally or by writing.

It is, in a word, the Central Committee which examines all projects with real care and minuteness, when not pressed by particular circumstances, and when composed of men who understand the subject, and work at it with a goodwill.

Sometimes the Central Committee is satisfied with the reasons given in the project of the Budget if they seem clear and satisfactory.

After discussing all the Articles and adopting the Budget as a whole, the Central Committee nominates a Reporter, whose duty it is to make a *résumé* of the discussion, and to explain and justify, if necessary, the conclusions adopted. The Reporter is often ordered by the Committee to confer with the Minister, either to arrive at an amicable solution of any given difficulties, or for the sake of obtaining additional explanations.

When the Report is drawn up it is read to the Committee, which approves, or it may be alters, adds to, or suppresses certain portions.

The Report as definitely approved by the Central Committee, is taken by the Reporter to the Chamber, and there laid on the table of the House, with the consent of the President.

The President then orders it to be printed, and distributed among the members of the House. According to its regulations two days must elapse after the distribution before the project can be discussed by the House itself. At least half the members must be present when the debate takes place—this rule has, however, been modified in practice, but no vote can take place unless half the members are present. After the general discussion on the Budget project as a whole, which may involve the general policy of the Government, under certain circumstances, the House passes on to the discussion of the separate articles. These are sometimes voted very rapidly, the President merely stating that no opposition is offered. Every member has a right to propose the rejection or modification of any article, or an amendment to it; and the President is obliged to entertain any such proposition if supported by at least five members. When all the articles have been adopted, whether in an amended form or not, the Budget is voted as a whole, each member replying "aye" or "no" as his name is called out. Any member can abstain from voting, but after the result of the voting is declared those who have abstained from voting must give their reasons for so doing.

The Budget as voted is sent up to the Senate, which then proceeds to deal with it. The Senate generally refers it to special Commissions, who name a special Reporter for each Budget. It is rarely that the Senate does more than take into consideration the Report made to the Chamber, and propose, it may be, rejections or amendments. I do not recollect any Budget being sent back to the Chamber by the Senate during the fourteen sessions in which I have been in Parliament.

Such are the constitutional formalities and regulations which allow in theory, if not in practice, all the members of the two Chambers to criticise, discuss, amend, or reject, not only each Budget as a whole, but each article of a particular Budget. But in Belgium, as no doubt in England and elsewhere, the practice is scarcely in accordance with the constitutional theory, laws, and regulations. I shall have occasion to refer to what is the practice in answering the other questions.

III. I have replied to this question above.

IV. All Committees can propose amendments to the projected Budget. They can equally propose the rejection of certain articles, or bring forward new ones. The written statement of proceedings mentions these proposals, their adoption, or rejection, by the Committee; the Central Committee examines them, discusses them, and, if necessary, submits them to the examination of the Minister whose department they affect, who gives his reasons, if he opposes the propositions in question. The Central Committee then decides if it shall uphold the proposed amendment before the House. This latter, after debate, decides whether or not it will sustain the amendment. The Senate can equally amend or reject the proposals which come to it from the Chamber, but cannot propose new sources of revenue, nor fresh expenditure; the initiative in these matters resides in the Chamber.

V. As I have said above, every Committee discusses the proposals as to receipts and expenditure submitted to the Chamber by the Government, independently of the other Committees. Some of these adopt the Budget proposals submitted to them without observation or discussion, whilst others discuss them at great length. In practice it is in the

Central Committee that takes place the full and detailed study and discussion of each Budget, each one of the members of this Committee bringing forward the opinion expressed in the particular Committee to which each member belongs. Even the opinions of the minority, or of a single member, are often recorded, either in the written statement of proceedings, or added to the Report as an appendix. Generally there are but few members who attend the Committees, because the discussions are poor, or because members are not versed in the subject, or because the matter is dealt with only as prepared by the Government or Minister.

VI. The laws and regulations of the Chamber make it absolutely necessary to send the Budgets to be examined by the Committees of the Chamber; it is only in cases of urgency, which very rarely occur, that the Chamber can submit the Budget to the examination of a special Commission appointed by the Chamber itself. The Central Committee is, in point of fact, a special Commission, nominated by the majority of the whole House, with the probability of the minority being represented in the Committee.

VII. It may be that if these lines are read in Belgium, some there will say that the writer of them is not sufficiently impartial to reply to this last question to which the ones which precede form a kind of prolegomena.

I have in fact always opposed increase of expenditure, especially of military expenditure. I have always opposed the construction, and above all the working of railways by the State, because this system is ever a permanently increasing cause of losses which have to be made good by the public treasury ; in a word I have, whatever ministry was in power, even when of my own party, invariably opposed the increase of the burdens of the country in general, and of the taxpayers in particular.

It will, therefore, be said that I am making a new speech in behalf of my favourite theme.

But whatever may be my personal position in the Belgian Parliament, which, in all honesty, I ought to mention to my colleagues of the Cobden Club, I must state my individual opinion in all sincerity and frankness, without prepossession, prejudice, or passion, basing my conclusions as much as possible on positive and incontestable facts.

I begin by allowing, what indeed it would be idle and unjust to deny, that the necessary intervention of the two Houses in the discussion and establishment of taxes and loans, and in the question of expenditure, has had generally the effect of preventing, at least temporarily, the reckless increase (*l'accroissement désordonné*) of imposts and expenditure ; but I say that it is doubtful, in my opinion, whether they have done so more efficaciously than would have been effected by the free exercise of public opinion without the intervention of the Chambers.

I have sometimes heard it said by old parliamentarians, without however agreeing to it myself, that a Government directly responsible to the taxpayers and the nation would be more careful of the public moneys than when it can discharge this responsibility on Chambers which represent the nation more or less faithfully.

This theory is also that of the partisans of absolute and uncontrolled power.

It may, however, be said with certainty to-day, I think, that experience has pronounced against this theory, for there is not a single absolutist Government which would dare confront, for a single month, the free exercise of public opinion. All the care and efforts of these Governments are above all concentrated upon the means of suppressing all discussion of their acts, and even every expression of opinion opposed to their own.

If parliaments had only the advantage of being an efficacious means of making various opinions known to the nation, and heard by it, they would be beneficent and indispensable institutions. Their discussions being more comprehensive, more enlightened, and more practical than those of the daily press, or of public meetings, are the true guide of public opinion. It is by these discussions that the nation is able to decide between the Opposition and the

Government, if the expression of public opinion is not falsified by vicious and fraudulent electoral practices.

It is not possible to lead astray public opinion for long where a free Parliament exists, which is the result of really free elections. I say thus much to show that if I cannot be accused of nourishing ideas hostile to a Government based on the parliamentary system, I am the better in a position to show that neither Belgium nor England completely realise in practice those constitutional and legal theories, of which I have pointed out the principles in my answers to the above questions.

In order that the system of control established in theory by the constitution and the laws should become a reality, the Ministry ought to be taken from the minority in the Parliament, and the opposition ought to form the real and effective majority. Then the question of taxation would be discussed without compromises, the expenditure would be thoroughly studied and scrutinised in its details; then it would be impossible for the central Committee to give up its judgment from one moment to another, because of Ministerial disapprobation.

But, unfortunately, the Government is taken from the majority; they mutually sustain each other, and, like the Siamese twins, they cannot be separated. The Government needs its majority; the majority equally needs *its* Government. Hence arise reciprocal compliance and mutual concessions, which throws out of gear the machinery of modern constitutions, constructed with such delicate care. The real result of this forced union of the majority with the Government is that the representatives of the taxpayers, instead of defending the interests of these latter at all times, and under all circumstances, are always ready to sacrifice those interests if the Government declare that it must have money, that it must impose such a tax, or incur a given expenditure. From that time control is a mere parliamentary comedy, played with more or less of skill and success. The Government banishes from the Central Committee competent and independent men ; the Reports are made with the concurrence (*concours*) of State Ministers and functionaries ; the opposition can only make itself heard when the matter is debated in full House, which listens out of politeness, the vote being decided beforehand, the Ministry having declared that it will give up office if the majority will not concede all the Government demands.

This cannot but startle and disappoint those who admire the mechanism, apparently so precise, of the Government *of* the country *by* the country, or, as the English say, "self-government."

The question must be more thoroughly gone into, and the real cause of this deception be got at, if the reason of this apparent anomaly is to be understood.

The two Chambers are nominated by electors legally qualified by the payment of a certain amount of direct taxes, fixed by the Constitution itself at the minimum of 42 francs 32 centimes, or about 37 shillings.

Belgium is divided, for the election of Members of Parliament, into electoral districts, in a manner the most anomalous (*bizarre*), the most unjust, and the most impolitic as regards the defence of the interests of the great mass of its taxpayers.

Some districts elect thirteen members, others seven, six, five, four, three, two, and even one only. One elector places thirteen names on his voting paper, another elector a single name. In one place an electoral district comprises sixteen or eighteen thousand electors, in another a district comprises only three hundred. The vote of two great liberal towns— Ghent and Antwerp—is drowned in the vote of peasants belonging to agricultural villages. These towns, important from their industry and commerce, are not represented in Parliament—or rather, the minority of their inhabitants are, while the majority are not. In other districts—Brussels for example—the rural populations are not represented in Parliament. In some districts, where the two parties are very evenly balanced, electoral corruption has taken root ; it seeks to create false electors, or to buy votes as cheaply as possible.

From the combination of these different elements, the electoral census and the distribution of seats in the electoral districts, arises the possibility, realised during the last six years, that a minority of electors can furnish a parliamentary majority, and even a strong one. Thus, 13 electoral districts, averaging 500 electors, or 6,500 altogether, of whom about 3,000 are of one opinion and 3,500 of the other, annul the electoral district, of Brussels for example, which also elects 13 deputies, the district having 17,000 or 18,000 electors, 13,000 being of one opinion and 5,000 of the other.

It is easy to understand, that in order to maintain such a state of things the majority has need of the help of the Government, and the Government must give it at any price, if it would preserve its majority.

Public works are the most costly but the surest means of forming or maintaining electoral majorities. These means are often used. On the other hand, the Government patronage is very great, since the working of railways, post-offices, and telegraphs employs 30,000 officials; and if different civil and military functionaries are added, as well as the bearers of honorary titles and decorations, or, again, Government contractors of various kinds, it may fearlessly be asserted that the action of the Government majority extends over 40,000 or 50,000 families, who influence more less the electors.

Now there are in Belgium only 115,000 electors who take part, or rather might take part, in the parliamentary elections ; as a matter of fact, 90,000 or 100,000 actually vote. Of this number a third if not one half, have an immediate interest in the increase of expenditure ; it is enough that they throw themselves into one scale or the other to turn the balance. The party which owes to them, at least in part, the possession of power, is necessarily grateful, so it is that when one party has given all it can, a turn is given to the other party, in order to get from it all that can be obtained in like manner. Hence it is that the deputies who oppose the current are few in number, and almost powerless. They can awaken public attention, keep it alive, and oblige the ministers to be relatively moderate, but the majority, urged by petitions and incessant demands constantly renewed, gets over this obstacle very often with the aid and even initiative of the opposition.

There is, then, no cause for astonishment if the direct taxes, which alone form the electoral basis, are only 40,000,000 in an expenditure of 256,000,000, and that consequently less than one-twelfth of the citizens of full age are electors. Only five years ago the majority did away with two direct taxes of a most justifiable character, the tax on tavern-keepers and on tobacco-sellers, because it supposed that their votes were generally unfavourable to the existing majority.

On the other hand the intrusion into our political affairs of an element totally foreign to it—I mean the religious question—has brought in a germ of animosity and passion which turns away a number of our electors from a healthy and reasonable idea of their true interests, and further diminishes the means of resistance to increased expenditure. The Roman Catholic clergy, stirred up by Rome, have thrown themselves resolutely into the electoral conflict. It persuades the more ignorant country people that those opposed to the clergy menace the people's religion, worship, churches, and priests ; that is enough to make the peasants vote blindly for those whom they are told to support, however prodigal they may be of the public money.

These remarks easily explain all the practical and economical conditions of the system. If the 115,000 electors divided among themselves the total produce of the taxes, revenues, customs, tolls, &c., they would each have 2,226 francs. Their contribution (*mise*) being less, on an average, than 300 francs, I calculate it in this way :—

One-third of the direct taxes (they certainly do not pay more)	14,000,000
One-twelfth of the remaining taxes	20,000,000
	34,000,000

This divided amongst 115,000 electors gives about 300 francs. But it is a majority of them which disposes of the resources of the State. This majority may be reduced by the combinations I have mentioned above to 40,000 or 45,000 voters, of whom many worthy persons are content with " the honour." It results then that the advantage of having the power permits the 40,000 or 45,000 who take part in the vote to divide among themselves a sum which would give each 5,000 francs, after all expenses deducted.

It is, then, no matter of astonishment that it is difficult in our country (Belgium) as in yours (England) to make economy and retrenchment prevail in the deliberations of Parliament. I have passed over, so as not to lengthen too much my proofs, the secondary influences which have the same tendency, and lead to the same results—the court, the army, the nobility, the principal functionaries, who add their influence in favour of expenditure, as well as influences I have already enumerated.

I shall perhaps be asked if I see a remedy for all this and an end to it. I frankly reply, No. The system must wear itself out as did that of Law in France in the last century.

If no foreign and disturbing element mixed itself up in the debates on our interests, perhaps public opinion, enlightened by discussion, would bring back the electors to the feeling of their responsibility towards those of whom they are the proper and responsible guardians, but the intervention of the religious element falsifies ideas, excites passions, and in fact remits the decision, touching expenses, to those classes of electors interested in swelling the Budget.

It must be remarked that numerous causes of augmentation of expenses are added every year to those which exist already.

Half the railways are not yet worked by the State; most of them are losing concerns, and ask to be bought up The State already loses considerably by working the prin cipal lines and those the most productive; what then will happen when it takes the less productive branches? It will be, however, obliged to take them, the principle being already laid down and accepted.

c

It is the same with telegraphs, post-offices, and steam-boats.

The State has undertaken the principal roads ; soon it will no doubt be asked to undertake the parish roads. Public instruction, behindhand as it is in the rural districts demands new sacrifices. Middle-class instruction is not sufficiently developed in centres of more or less importance ; loans will be effected to cover this expense, and interest will be added to the interest paid for preceding loans. Numbers of influential people urge the Government to borrow money. They seem to think that the public treasury fills itself without further effort.

The increase of expense is then inevitable, and that for a long time to come.

Perhaps some day the agricultural classes will perceive that they alone bear the chief expense of these augmentations, and then, if they can agree with the commercial and manufacturing classes, one may hope for a Chamber decided to carry out economy.

But the chance is but a small one. We are going, then, to absorb for State expenditure the total amount of the revenue of real property, land and houses included. When this has been done perhaps the Government itself will deem it wise not to break in on other revenues.

A prolonged crisis might force us, sooner than we think, to be more prudent, and therefore more economical.

When that time comes—may it come without a crisis—the Committees will choose for Reporters competent men instead of easy-going men, they will be chosen without too much consideration for their special phase of political opinion, and the country will be all the better for it.

As I hope I have shown, the instrument itself is good, the constitutional machine lacks but little, it is only the firm determination to make proper use of it that is wanted.

It is to be hoped that here in Belgium, as elsewhere, the necessity for so doing will soon be felt.

Accept, sir, the expression of my esteem.

(Signed)　　Ad. le Hardy de Beaulieu.

T. B. Potter, Esq., M.P.

DENMARK.

SUMMARY.

I. Every year, at the opening of the Session of the States-General in September, the Government is obliged to bring forward a complete and very detailed Budget for the ensuing year, together with an account of the sums received and paid out during the last two years. If in the course of the year any unforeseen wants arise, the Government has to propose a special Budget.

II. The financial measures of the Government are first laid before the Lower House. Its members divide themselves into five Special Committees or Sections for the preparatory examination of the Budget. Each Section nominates a Reporter. These five Reporters collect and discuss the observations brought forward in each Section, and communicate with the Minister by a Report, called the " Preparatory Report." The Minister replies by another Report, in which he maintains the provisions of his Budget as against the remarks of the Sections, or modifies his proposals in accordance with their remarks. By this exchange of Reports the subject is duly prepared for public discussion in the House itself, each member of which can state his opinion, or propose any amendment he deems right.

The conferences which take place between the Ministers and Finance Committee are of great importance in clearing up and modifying the proposals made. The Chamber almost always decides in favour of the report drawn up by the Reporter of the Finance Committees. When the Budget is passed either with or without amendment by the Lower House, it goes to the Upper House, where it is examined in the same manner, first in the sections or committees, and afterwards by the whole House.   In case the two Houses differ about the Budget, a joint committee can be formed to make proposals leading to an agreement.   What should be done if such agreement cannot be effected is the great question of the day in Denmark between the Government supported by the Upper House on one side, and the great majority of the Lower House on the other.   The latter claims full rights as regards parliamentary government and Ministerial responsibility.

III. The Budget must be divided into several heads, representing the several departments of the public service, and the various expenses of each department can also be further divided under separate heads.   The present divisions are

  1. Crown Expenditure.

  2. Expenditure of great public bodies called " High Colleges of State," viz :   The States-General. Council of State, &c.

  3. Foreign Department.

  4. Law.

  5. Home.

  6. Naval.

7*a*. National Debt.

7*b*. Finance.

  8. War.

  9. Colonies.

10. Allowance for unforeseen contingencies not to exceed 100,000 florins.

Each of these heads has its own sub-divisions arranged in chapters, paragraphs, and articles, with a maximum for every single article.   The members of the Lower House discuss each article.

IV. The conclusions arrived at by the Sections or Committees are subject to the decision of the whole House.

V. The Constitution of Denmark secures sufficiently the independence of the Legislature, and of the Committees appointed by them ; these latter are selected by ballot, care being taken that the minority should have a voice in them.

VI. The disbursements in conformity with the Budget, as finally approved, are controlled by a Committee of Revision, composed of four members, two for each House. The work of the Revision Committee is approved by the Chambers before being handed over to the Court of Accounts (*Rekenkamer*). The members of this latter body are appointed for life by the Crown out of a list nominated by the Lower Chamber.

VII. The course pursued in regulating the Budget has proved very efficacious in keeping down charges recommended by the Government, and the effect in limiting expenditure has been very salutary.

Statement of M. FREDERICKSEN, *Professor of Political Economy at the University of Copenhagen.*

A VERY detailed Budget is, with full explanatory details, at the beginning of the yearly session, ordinarily in the month of October, laid before the House of Commons. At the first reading the Budget is discussed generally by the Minister of Finance, and is the occasion on which members state views of the most different nature. After the first reading a member will propose the election of the Financial Committee, of late consisting of fifteen members, the present majority always preferring large committees. The Committee is—as most of the other Committees of the Parliament—elected by ballot, and is in accordance with the particular method of election of minorities introduced here so early as 1855, by Mr. Andrae. This Financial Committee has the most important Parliamentary work, and is not unjustly called "the most influential body of the realm." Especially the Reporter—I do not know if I may use the English term "Speaker"—of this Committee, is of the greatest influence. Of the full independence of the Committee there can be no

question with us.   Even when the Government party was in
a majority, the Committee worked quite independently; now
it pays, perhaps, even more regard to the opinion of the
electors.   The Financial Committee is ordinarily divided
into sub-committees, each of two members, for the several
departments.   It begins its work by putting a great many
questions in writing to the Government Departments.   The
sub-committees report their special heads to the Committee;
a Reporter for the whole Budget, or for its different parts, is
returned, and, finally, the Reporter draws up a Report to the
Chamber.   This Report is first printed for private cir-
culation, and a preliminary supervision takes place within
the Committee.   Then conferences are usually held with
the different members of the Cabinet—conversations which
are often of main importance for the Administration, and of
great influence on the ultimate votes of the Committee.
At last the Report is finally voted in the Committee, and
printed for the Chamber and the public.   At the succeeding
second reading the Chamber almost always votes with the
majority of the Committee.   At the third and last reading
the Government will especially repeat the motions to which it
attaches some importance.   The consideration of the Budget
by the Committee of the lower House (Folkething), and by
the Chamber itself, generally taking up almost the whole
time of the session, the Budget will often be transmitted
very late to the upper House—the Landsthing—where it is
also often very hurriedly read three times.   Very often the
Government employs the Landsthing in order to get rid
of the most disagreeable amendments put in by the
Folkething.   The Landsthing itself makes it an essential
point to repel the attempts of the other House to alter, by
means of the Budget, what is organised by special bills, the
Lower House, in fact, having a prominent influence on the
Budget, not on the Bills.   In case of the two Chambers
finally differing, a joint committee can be formed to make
proposals for an agreement.   Supposing the two Chambers
are unable to arrive at such agreement, what then is to be
done?   That is, at the present moment, the great political

question in Denmark between the Ministry supported by the Upper House on the one side, and the great majority of the Lower House on the other side. In settling this question, the latter body aspires to and claims parliamentary government.

The present very detailed form of the Budget was introduced the first year of our constitution by Mr. Fenger, then a celebrated physician, for several years Reporter of the Financial Committee, afterwards Minister of Finance, now burgomaster of Copenhagen. He took his model for the main part from the Budget of Christian VIII. of the year 1841, the absolute government of this king having on the whole, by its administrative reforms, greatly prepared the way for our constitution. At the period when we, owing to the controversy with Germany, had two constitutions, one for the monarchy and one for the kingdom proper, and at one time even absolute government in the matters of the monarchy, the Budget had different forms at different times.

A Budget—called "Normal Budget"—was fixed, and supplementary grants were voted for each two years. It must be especially mentioned that at this period Mr. Andrae did away with many details in the Budget. After the loss of the duchies we returned again to a less complicated method. In the Budget we again took up the old more detailed form. Yet I should say that Mr. Fenger himself would now admit that it would be better without so many details, and that this might be preferable even as regards constitutional responsibility.

I don't think our mode of dealing with the Budget the most perfect. Much depends certainly on the characters of the members of the Committee, especially of the Chairman and of the Reporter. Formerly our ablest men, as Mr. Monrad, Mr. Tscherninz, Mr. Fenger, have filled these places. Lately, Mr. Fenger being a member of the Ministry, we had, for a short period, the more important duties of Reporter divided amongst several of us. At present, the party of peasants being in the majority, Mr. Berz, originally a village teacher, has for some years been the Reporter, and thereby the bearer of a great deal of our parliamentary work. He is certainly not without capacity, but on the other hand he is perhaps not without blame for the extreme length of the debates both in the Committee and in the House. The casual Committee has a very great power, and I don't think our way of forming Committees by election is very good; the election for the Committees—to which much importance is attached by members from the personal honour belonging to it—and not least, the elections by the method of minorities do not act salutarily on the formation of our political parties, neither do they produce the best working Committees. As our Financial Committee works, it very often attaches over-much importance to the details, even rather more than to the great financial questions; it does not unfrequently torment the Government departments with details, and rather unimportant questions, and I have sometimes had a strong impression of our doing more harm than good with our Committee work. I think it would be better not to revise every year all the details of the Budget, and I would prefer separate Committees appointed for examining each their separate heads of the Budget, instead of the voluminous correspondence of our Financial Committee. I should prefer the method of verbally inquiring, as in the case of your Select Committees.

The full and elaborate state accounts, as well as the reports of our state-auditors, are to be seen by the forwarded copies. The four auditors are elected every year, two by each House; their election is often considered as a reward for political merits to their party, According to the report of the auditors the accounts for the year following are decided on by votes of the Chambers. Instead of the much retarded and not very efficient supervision of the auditors, I should certainly prefer a Court of Accounts of Belgian model.

It must be admitted that our public economy on the whole is very good, and that this is greatly owing to the Financial Committee, as also to the "Folkething" itself. It ought, however, to be mentioned, that many new expenses are granted by special bills. It often happens that the House is willing to vote even large amounts in this way, more readily than in the Budget; especially as the Government not unfrequently, by means of Royal Commissions, including influential members of the Houses, succeeds in getting great expenses through the House. Upon the whole the House is nevertheless very economical; yet I should ascribe the merit of our public economy to our very Democratic Constitution rather than to our special way of dealing with the Budget. The majority in this country is with the peasants, peasant-proprietors, and land-holders; the labourers follow the peasant proprietors, and, as in Sweden and Norway, and contrary to the rest of Europe, they also themselves sit in the Chamber. Our wide electoral franchise in Denmark produces a majority certainly not the most intelligent, and perhaps even more demagogical than in the other Scandinavian countries, because we have the complete " suffrage universel," as at present in France ; the difference between the two Chambers is also a great difficulty ; but the peasant majority has certainly the chief merit of our public economy. They vote readily for great expenses to railways and schools for the people, but they seldom incline to vote for salaries exceeding their own very low estimated incomes. Our Government officers are better paid than for instance in Prussia, yet the economical situation in Denmark is at present such that the supply of candidates for office is now much reduced; under the former absolute Government every intelligent man aspired to a "secure" place in a Government office. It may perhaps come to this here as in Holland, that almost only well-to-do people can take office. Upon the whole this might, however, not be to the prejudice of our social progress. Still more interesting for the finances are the military expenses. The proposed military grants, very considerable for our small country, will find but slight resistance from our intelligent classes, subject to the influence of the military and whole official body ; also the grants for our literary men, " the glory of the country," are commonly considered of more consequence than eco-

nomy. But our farmers are upon the whole not inclined
to grant money for expensive military institutions, and
they particularly dislike to lay down great capital in
fortifications. Considering the situation of our little
country, I don't think they are mistaken. Of great
administrative "abuses" we have none in Denmark; many
reforms were introduced in 1848, the year of our constitution, many are certainly yet to be taken in hand; but now,
with our peasants' party in the majority and in opposition to
the Government, very few new expenses are voted by the
Lower House; on the other hand almost no administrative
reforms are carried out by the present Conservative ministry.
The majority of the Chamber, at present in opposition,
is still more disposed to economy than it would be if it
formed the Government; the Cabinet on the other hand
being in a minority in this Chamber seeks almost only to
resist the reformers. Our whole stationary situation is
indeed far from being agreeable. For their economical
opposition I can however forgive our peasant majority
many political faults.

Reply of COUNT SPONNECK, *Director of the National Bank,*
Copenhagen.

I. In the greatest detail, and with very circumstantial
explanations.

II. The items proposed by Government or by the members of the Legislature, having an unlimited right of initiative,
are discussed *ad libitum*, partly in full Assembly, and partly
in Committees selected by the Assembly.

III. Sometimes they are, and sometimes they are not,
according to the choice of the Assembly.

IV. The Ministers of the Crown are admitted to make
observations, but the decisions and proposals of the Committee are only subject to revision and alteration by the
Assembly.

V. The Constitution of Denmark secures sufficiently the

independence of the Legislature and the Committees against any attempt from the Government to check them or to abuse them.

VI. The national expenditures and their conformity with the Budget approved by the Legislature are controlled by a Committee of Revision (the " Statsrevision ") composed of four members, two selected by each Chamber (the " Folke-thing " and the " Landsthing "). The proposals of the " Statsrevision " are submitted to and approved by the Chambers before quittance is given to the State accounts of each year.

VII. The course pursued by the legislative body in Denmark (the " Rigsdag ") has in experience proved most efficacious, and sometimes rather too efficacious in keeping down the charges recommended by Government. The effect of limiting abuses in administration has been very salutary.

W. SPONNECK.

Copenhagen, July 6th, 1876.

FRANCE.

SUMMARY.

I. The Government, at the beginning of the annual Session, presents, in the form of a volume, the details of expenditure as proposed for the next ensuing year. Thus, the estimates of expenditure for 1877 were laid on the table of the Assembly in March, 1876. It contained: 1st, a financial statement by the Minister of Finance; 2nd, a Bill, divided into twenty-two Sections, with seven schedules; viz.,

a. General estimate of the expenditure.
b. Schedule of the taxes to be levied in 1877.
c. Sums to be paid by each Department as land-tax, personal tax, or tax on doors and windows.
d. Schedule of the rates, duties, rents, authorised to be levied.
e. General Statement of ways and means.
f. Receipts of expenditure from special funds.
g. Special accounts.

There is also in the volume a general statement of the Budget of the year, a comparison between the sums to be collected and those to be expended; the Budget of the last year is compared with the previous year; and there is a statement concerning the unconsolidated or floating debt. This last part contains a very detailed estimate of the receipts and expenditure. The items of expenditure are given separately for each of the public departments :—

1. Justice and Public Worship.
2. Foreign Office.
3. Home Department and Algeria.
4. Finances.
5. War Office.
6. Admiralty and Colonies.
7. Public Education.
8. Agriculture and Trade.
9. Public Works.

II. The National Assembly elects a Budget Committee of 33 members. It is divided into sub-divisions, each of which examines one or two of the Budgets of different State Departments. Everything is laid before the Budget Committee in full detail, and the Finance Ministers and other official persons attend to give explanations and information. A Reporter is nominated by the Committee to draw up a special report of the Budget. When the Budget Committee has finished its work, it lays its conclusions before the Assembly in the shape of one or more Reports, which are printed and distributed. After this comes the discussion of the Budget in full Assembly. There is a discussion of the Budget as a whole, and then one on each of its various details. Every item of expenditure is voted separately. Every member has a right of proposing amendments, either with a view to increase or diminish expenditure.

The Government has, of course, the same right, and naturally combats more or less any changes proposed by the Budget Committee. The vote of the Assembly determines the final form which the Budget is to take. The same rules apply to the mode in which the Senate deals with the Budget; but the Senatorial Committee of the Budget is composed of only eighteen members.

III. The Budget is divided into as many parts as there are Ministers, and the expenditure of each Ministry is divided into various chapters and sections. The whole is laid before the Committee, but it is customary, as has been said above, to subdivide the Budget Committee, and give to each sub-division the Budget of a particular department to examine.

IV. The decisions come to by the Committee, or by its sub-divisions, have no legal force in themselves. The Assembly decides everything by its votes, either for or against the proposals of the Government, of the Budget Committee, or of individual deputies.

V. Although the vote of the Committee has no legal force unless adopted by the Assembly, the Committee has the fullest liberty and authority for fulfilling its mission, which is that of examining the Budget in all its details, questioning all officials, and formulating the conclusions which are proposed to the Assembly.

VI. As the Budget Committee is always appointed with special power to deal with the Budget itself, and as each Deputy preserves his right of proposing amendments in the Assembly, no other special means are wanted or provided.

VII. The system of dealing with the Budget actually in operation in France gives a most effective control over Government expenditure. But private members have the right of proposing fresh expenditure or additional credits. The financial equilibrium proposed by the Government may therefore be compromised by such proposals, or by those of the Budget Committee, but it rests with the Legislature to determine in every case what course should be adopted.

One of the most important parts of the French financial system is that of the *Cour des Comptes* (Court of Accounts), composed of eminent magistrates who, as a supreme tribunal, take care that every item of expenditure should be accompanied by a sufficient authorisation according to the forms prescribed by law. All actual payments have to be made and approved by this *Cour des Comptes*. It is no longer allowed to transfer expenses or payments from one department to another, as was often done under the second Empire.

Letter from M. Léon Say, *Minister of Finance.*

Paris, 8th July, 1876.

Sir,—I have the honour of sending you, with this, a note, replying, as regards France, to the printed questions of the Cobden Club, touching the means of control applicable to the public expenditure.

The rules which regulate the presentation and the discussion of our Budgets having been shown in a very complete manner by a certain number of authors, the following replies have been limited to the seven questions put forward by the Cobden Club circular.

Accept, sir, &c., &c.,

(Signed)   Léon Say,

Minister of Finance.

T. B. Potter, Esq., M.P.,
Hon. Sec. of the Cobden Club.

Replies of M. Léon Say.

I. The Government, at the commencement of the annual session of Parliament, lays on the table of the Chamber of Deputies the projected Budget of the following year, comprising, together with the enumeration of the taxes and dues, whose levying has been authorised, the indication of the presumed yield of each one of them, and the details of the credits asked for the ordinary and extraordinary expenses of the different ministries or departments.

The projected Budget is printed, and then distributed among all the members of Parliament.

It is discussed and voted, first by the Chamber of Deputies, and then by the Senate.

II. Every projected law presented to the Chamber of Deputies is subjected to the following procedure :—

The Chamber is divided each month, by lot, into eleven equal groups called (*Bureaux*) Committees, each Committee discusses the project summarily, and then nominates one or two (*Commissaires*) Commissioners or Reporters, according to the importance of the project.

The union of the eleven, twenty-two, or thirty-three Commissioners so nominated, forms the Commission, which is charged with the thorough examination of the project and of proposed amendments.   It then presents a Report.

This general procedure is applicable to the project of a Budget.   The Budget Commission is composed of thirty-three members, and is divided into several sub-committees.

When the Budget Commission has done its work, it lays its conclusions before the Chamber in the shape of Reports, duly printed and distributed.

Not until then does the discussion, in full Assembly, commence.

It must be added, that to the Budget Commission are sent all the Government projects touching demands of credit, supplementary or extraordinary, belonging to current account, and all Government projects of law and all propositions emanating from the initiative of Parliament, whose object is to modify the revenue or expenditure of the State.

Thus, no fresh expenditure or augmentation of expense can escape the control of the Budget Commission.

The same rules are applicable to the discussion of the Budget by the Senate, but the Senate's Budget Commission is composed of only eighteen members.

III. The expenditure of the Budget project is divided into as many parts as there are Ministries, and into chapters and articles for each Ministry.

The whole is sent to the same Commission, but it is the custom, as has been shown, that the Budget Commission should be divided into as many sub-committees as there are ministries and departments.

In the Chamber of Deputies, for example, the Budget Commission of 1877, actually (July, 1876) in session, is divided into five sub-committees :—

1. Sub-committee on finance.
2. Sub-committee for home, Algerian, and foreign affairs.
3. Sub-committee for war and marine.
4. Sub-committee for justice, public worship, education, and fine arts.
5. Sub-committee for public works, agriculture, and commerce.

The vote on the Budget is taken chapter by chapter.

IV. The decisions come to by the Budget Commission have not of themselves any legal value; the Chamber has the full right of voting. The Government can obtain in "full Assembly" credits of which the Budget Commission has obtained the suppression; so also the authors of the amendments to the Budgets can get their proposals maintained, despite the adverse conclusion of the Commission.

V. The votes of the Budget Commission are, as has been shown, without legal effect, and merely recommend to the Assembly a given conclusion. But the Commission has all the authority necessary to the fulfilment of the work confided to it. It can oblige the Ministers to give every necessary explanation.

VI. This question is not in any way applicable to the French procedure.

VII. The system actually in force in France, subjects to a very efficient control both the Government and Administration, as to the necessity and utility of the credits demanded. Unfortunately, it is not forbidden in France, as in England, for Members of Parliament to take upon themselves, by means of amendments or proposals, the initiative of fresh expenditure, or augmentation of credits. The equilibrium prepared by the Government runs the risk, therefore, of being compromised by those very persons whose proper mission should be that of restraining the public administration, in the matter of expenditure, instead of encouraging the augmentation of its Budgets.

D

M. DE FRANQUEVILLE *writes from Paris,* 12*th July,* 1876.

DEAR SIR,—I received your note on my return to Paris, and I have the honour to send you the answers to the various questions relating to the French system of voting the public expenditure.

I shall gladly supply you with any further information you might require on my return from Switzerland by the end of September.

Believe me, dear sir, yours very truly,

(Signed) FRANQUEVILLE.

T. B. POTTER, Esq., M.P.

Replies of M. DE FRANQUEVILLE.

The Government sends to the National Assembly, as soon as possible after the commencement of the session, a very large volume (printed by the national printing office, under the supervision of the *Ministre des Finances*) containing in detail the proposed items of expenditure for the next ensuing year. For instance, the volume containing the estimates for the year 1877 (January 1st to December 31st) was placed upon the table of the National Assembly on the 14th of March, 1876. It is entitled, *Projet de loi pour la fixation des recettes et des dépenses de l'exercice* 1877. It contains first a financial statement (*exposé des motifs*) by the Minister of Finance; second, a bill (*projet de loi*), divided into twenty-two sections (*articles*) with seven schedules (*tableaux*), viz.—

a. General estimate of the expenditure.
b. Schedule of the taxes to be levied in 1877.
c. Sums to be paid by each Department as land-tax, personal tax, and tax on doors and windows.
d. Schedule of the rates, duties, and rents authorised to be levied.
e. General statement of ways and means.
f. Receipts and expenditure out of special funds.
g. Special accounts.

The same volume contains besides, a general annotation on the Budget of the year, a comparison between the sums to be collected and those to be expended; the Budget of the last year is compared with that of the present year, with a statement on the unconsolidated debt.

The last part, consisting of no less than 1,220 pages, contains a very detailed estimate of the receipts and expenditure.

The items of expenditure are given separately for each of the public departments.

1. Justice and Public Worship.
2. Foreign Office.
3. Home Department and Algeria.
4. Finances.
5. War Office.
6. Admiralty and Colonies.
7. Public Education and Art.
8. Agriculture and Trade.
9. Public Works.

It may be added that the *Budget* of every department is divided into a large number of *Articles*, which have to be voted separately.

Until the close of the Imperial Government, the Budget was voted, first by the Council of State, secondly by the Legislative Body, thirdly by the Senate. Under the system now in force it is only necessary that it should be voted by the National Assembly and by the Senate.

As soon as the Budget is placed upon the table, the National Assembly appoints a special Committee (*Commission du Budget*), which is subdivided into a certain number of sub-committees. Every sub-committee is required to examine the items of expenditure of one or two public departments. The attendance of the Minister or other officials appointed every year as commissioners of the Government (*Commissaires du Gouvernement*), is necessary in order to obtain the requisite information and explanations, they also examine the various amendments which may be proposed by the members of the Assembly. This examination being completed, a Reporter is appointed, and he is charged with the drawing up of the special report.

The Report is first read before the sub-committee, and, if approved, is also read before the full Committee. Besides the special reports containing the resolutions and recommendations for each of the public departments, a general Report is also made by a member of the Committee, in order to explain the general economy of the Budget.

When the general and special reports have been deposited upon the table, a day is appointed for a discussion of them in full Assembly. There is firstly what is styled a general discussion—that is to say, a discussion on the financial policy of the Government; then follows the discussion of the various parts of the Budget.

Every item of expenditure is voted separately, and every member is allowed to propose, as an amendment, either the increase or diminution of the sum proposed by the Committee. The Government has, of course, the same right, and exercises it, particularly in order to obtain the vote of the sum which has been inserted in the estimates, when this sum has been reduced by the Committee.

It must be noticed that the general principle of the English Constitution that no money may be voted, no grant increased, without a special recommendation from the Government, is not admitted by the French law, so that every member has the right to propose and the Assembly the right to vote any sum it likes without limitation.

I should add that it has been found from experience that the course pursued by the National Assembly has not the effect of keeping down the charges recommended by the the Government, or of limiting abuses in administration.

Statement of M. DE FONPERTUIS.

I. There is no time fixed for presenting the Budget (receipts and expenses). It is, however, habitually presented at the beginning of the parliamentary session, and it is obligatory in this sense that the Government cannot avoid doing it at one time or another of the said session.

When the Budget project has once been presented to the Chamber, it is inserted, with the explanatory and preliminary report, "*son exposé de motifs,*" in the official journal.

This statement brings out the increase or diminution of the credits asked for, and justifies them. It also gives an account of the increase or decrease which has been manifested in the receipts of the preceding Budget considered as the basis for the estimates and prevision of the succeeding Budget.

The expenditure (*Budget des Dépenses*) is the subject of a separate volume, which must be distributed among the deputies and senators, and of which the public papers find no difficulty in procuring copies for themselves.

II. The expenditure is voted, by the whole legislative body, section by section, chapter by chapter, article by article, in the case of each ministry: Foreign affairs, agriculture and commerce, war, public instruction, interior or home department, justice, marine, and public works.

But each of the Chambers nominates a Budget commission, which can, as is usually done, divide itself into sub-commissions, which divide amongst themselves the examination of the different ministries, and prepare separate reports, proposing for each branch of the public service the increase or diminution of expense which they consider useful.

III. The above details answer this third question as well as the second.

IV. The Budget Commission, or its sub-commissions, examine Ministers whose expenditure it is proposed to diminish. If the Minister consents, that ends the matter, except indeed as regards the supreme authority of the Chambers, which can always accept or reject the proposals of their Commissions.

If the Minister refuses, the question comes before the Chambers, which, by its vote, decides in favour of the Ministers or of the Commissions.

The revision of the decisions of the Budget Commissions belongs then to the Chambers.

The Government has only the right of being heard, and of making its proposal prevail, if it can, by argument.

V. Such independence has been secured by the Budget Commission having the right to demand of the Ministers and heads of departments such explanations as the Commission judges necessary for the accomplishment of its duty, and the execution of its work.

If the Commission should encounter any opposition in this matter, it must lay the matter before the Chamber, which has the power to settle it.

VI. This question is answered by what has gone before.

VII. This question may, generally speaking, be answered by a decided negative; at least, as concerns France, whose expenditure has not ceased increasing for fifty years, especially from 1852—1870.

Different causes explain this fact. Under the Government of July (Louis Philippe) a strong impulse was given to public works, and was continued under the Empire. This latter had, moreover, the most uneconomical ways (*habitudes*) possible; it took pride in doing things after a grand fashion, and dilapidated the finances. A servile Senate and a Legislative Body, nominated apparently by universal suffrage, in reality by the Prefects, were naturally not likely to stand in the way of this prodigality. These Assemblies did not discuss the Budget, they only voted it. The single Assembly which took their place from 1870 to 1876, in order to fill a gulf, and at the same time to re-establish a military condition completely destroyed, had to impose one of the heaviest Budgets ever brought forward.

The Budget for the navy has been really reduced; that of the army, on the contrary, has been notably increased. In this matter no economy can be looked for for a long time. The Government does not dream of it, nor would the Chambers or the country consent, if it did think of it. All that one sees is a large field open to future economies, that would be a bold initiative as regards administration,

but we are, as has often been said, too much administered.
In this matter the Government alone is not in fault; the
so-called directing classes are its accomplices, greedy of
place for their relations and dependents; parents, too, instead of putting their children into business and commerce,
prefer turning them into little official personages.

The actual Chamber is animated with the best intentions
as to reform ; but one cannot ask it to do impossibilities.
It will require years of good government and of the true
republican spirit before it is possible either to reform (*re-
manier*) our fiscal machinery (which is far from conforming
to sound economical principles, and which is composed of
heterogenous parts superposed and joined one to another as
best may be), or to lay the axe to our administrative system
now so thickly overgrown.

(Signed)   A. DE FONPERTUIS.

Letter from M. MAURICE BLOCK.

Paris, 2 July, 1876.

SIR,—By your printed circular of the 28th June, 1876,
you do me the honour of asking me various questions as to
the means adopted in France for criticising and controlling
the expenditure proposed by the Executive Government.

Although much occupied at this moment, I hasten to
reply to your questions without entering into details.

I. In the first months of each year the Government submits to the Chamber of Deputies the project of a Budget
for the following year; thus, in January or February, 1876,
was submitted the projected Budget for 1877. This project
is very detailed, at least as much so as your estimates : it
is a very thick blue book.

II. The discussion of the Budget takes place, as in the
case of every projected law, first in a Special Commission
elected by the Chamber. This Commission is sub-divided
into various Committees. The Report is first discussed in
committee and then defended before the Chamber.

III. Yes. Generally there is a Committee to examine the expenses of each Ministry, and a Special Committee touching receipts. The Commission is sub-divided as itself thinks best.

IV. The Budget Commission—of which the committees or sub-commissions are only sub-divisions—does not decide anything definitely ; it confines itself to proposing to the Chamber a given reduction or increase, as it thinks fit. Generally it calls before it the ministers or heads of department, and discusses modifications of the Budget with them, but this discussion has no other object than that of enlightening the members of the Commission.

In the Chamber the Minister and each deputy may attack or defend the Report of the Commission, or the proposals of the Government, as well as present amendments. New amendments—that is, those which have not been seen by the Commission—are sent back to it before any discussion takes place, so that the Commission may give its opinion.

In general, the views of the Commission are adopted by the Chamber ; sometimes the Commission remains in a minority on a given question.

V. This question does not seem to me very clear—at least, from the French point of view. If you ask me in what degree the Commission can come to a definite decision, I reply—It is not charged with taking definite decisions ; it is the general assembly of the Chamber which decides the matter. The Commission proposes, the Chamber votes.

If, however, you refer to the independence of individuals, I can only say there is no "arrangement" necessary for it— it is an affair of honour and honesty.

VI. As there is a Commission this question requires no reply. I will, however, add that the laws concerning the public accounts (*la comptabilité publique*) put a certain check on exaggerated expenses, but this check is not very strong.

The Budget is voted by articles, and the Government cannot change the articles. An article is a "vote," a law. The Treasury only allows, for each item of expense, the amount allowed under that head. We say, in French, "*le montant du crédit ouvert*"—the amount of the credit allowed.

VII. Your seventh question is very vague ; it would require a volume to answer it properly. Here are, in two words, the result of my studies :—In every country, without exception, the expenditure increases little by little, and that cannot be otherwise, since the population increases, and wants augment. But it is very probable that the Budget increases more quickly than is necessary. As to abuses, they are to be found everywhere ; you may diminish them, but you cannot make them disappear. Why? Because the amount of a future expense is a matter of valuation or appreciation, and an eloquent Minister will make a majority vote almost anything he wishes.

I beg you, sir, to be good enough to consider this short reply as a proof of my desire to fall in with your wishes.

Believe me, &c., &c.,

(Signed)   MAURICE BLOCK.

T. B. POTTER, Esq., M.P.

Letter from M. COFFINIÈRES.

Paris, July, 1876.

SIR,—In reply to the letter which you did me the honour to address to me last June, and which a prolonged absence prevented my receiving up to this time, I hasten to give you the following information in the order in which your questions are put :—

I. Immediately on the opening of the Legislative Session, the general work is subdivided among nine committees (*bureaux*) whose presidents and secretaries are nominated by the majority. One of these Committees is specially devoted to the Budget of Expenditure (*Budget des Dépenses*), a document which is at once laid on the President's table by the Finance Minister. This projected Budget also includes every kind of receipt devoted to the profit of the

State. It gives a *résumé* of the financial condition of all the Ministries, and is divided into special chapters. The law forbids the application to any one chapter, by a transfer of funds, of the credits opened for any other chapter.

II. It is in the Budget Commission itself, and before any public debate in the Chamber, that the different heads of expenditure are discussed. The Commission has the right to call before it the Ministers who can furnish the explanations which it needs.

III. The opinions formulated by the members of the Budget Commission, and the decisions come to by them form the subject of a very minutely detailed report, by the most competent member of the Commission. This report is read in public sitting, and it is ordered to be printed for distribution to each Deputy.

IV. The Chamber alone, by a majority of votes, can modify the expenses set down in the Ministerial project.

V. The most complete independence is secured to all the members of the Budget Commission; but this does not prevent their being influenced by the Ministers who seek to modify, as they deem best, the opinions of the Commission.

No Government abstains from using such means as it has at its disposal for this object.

VI. One of the best means of controlling State expenditure resides in the right possessed by all the papers, without distinction, to discuss the question; and as each party is represented in the Chamber by a larger or smaller number of the members of the Budget Commission, it follows that before being debated legislatively the expenditure has been discussed, as has been said, by the whole press.

VII. To these different elements of control it is only just to attribute the extreme prudence with which each Minister fixes the expenditure of his department. This method has contributed much to prevent civil, military, and naval prodigality.

Finally, one of the most remarkable parts of the French financial system is the Court of Accounts or Audit Office (*la Cour des Comptes*). It is composed of eminent magistrates, who sit as a supreme tribunal, and see that each item of expense is sanctioned by a voucher drawn up in due form, as prescribed by the finance laws.

I shall be happy if this information meets your wishes,

And I remain, &c.,

(Signed)   COFFINIÈRES.

T. B. POTTER, Esq., M.P.

Letter from M. GUSTAVE D'EICHTAL.

July, 1876.

DEAR SIR,—The circular signed by you relative to the control of public expenditure reached me a few days back at Carlsbad. I have never attended to practical politics, and should be somewhat embarrassed to reply exactly to the questions of the Cobden Club. I can, however, perfectly tell you that, given the actual state of things in Europe and in France, I do not see what other control could be exercised over public expenditure than that of Parliamentary control. In France this control is exercised by the Budget Commission of the Chamber of Deputies, and by the sub-commissions into which it is divided. This control is more or less real or effective (*sérieux*) according as the Chamber is more or less independent of the central power, and according as it has more or less initiative. Under the Empire, and indeed until the election of the actual Chamber, this control was *nil*, or simply nominal; the fear of offending had a restraining influence up to a certain point. In the present House, M. Gambetta being nominated a member, and then President of the Budget Commission, gave it an importance to which indeed it had a natural tendency.

But to tell you my real opinion, I think that all the efforts to moderate public expenditure will be powerless so long as the general spirit and tendency of society are not changed, so long as a condition or state of peace—organised peace—among the nations does not take the place of a

state of war, or even of armed peace.   In the name of
safety and of national glory Governments will always be
drawn, even against their will, to demand sacrifices from
the people which they will not dare refuse.   Besides, war is
a school of waste and disorder, and it is very difficult for
administrations whose object is military power not to be
more or less affected by such (evil) tendencies.

The remedy of all this (but it cannot be applied immediately) is that society, from the material point of view,
should consider itself a great productive workshop, a great
industrial society, which like all similar societies, enriches
itself by work, economy, and the good management of its
resources.   In this matter the commercial world itself has
something to learn.   Since the beginning of the century it
seems to me to dispose of the national resources of the
world as if it considered them unlimited.   But this is not
however the case.   Before long, I think, this will be recog-
nised, as it is already being seen that war, as now waged,
costs too much to be a pleasure that can long be indulged.
The world will thus be led to organise that great society
of labour, which was the dream of my master St. Simon,
as it was that of Cobden, and the realisation of which
actual events tend to hasten.

I remain, dear sir, &c. &c.,

(Signed)   GUSTAVE D'EICHTAL.

T. B. POTTER, Esq., M.P.

GERMANY.

SUMMARY.

I. The Government of the German Empire and of the Prussian State is obliged, before the commencement of every political year, to lay before the Parliament a detailed estimate of the whole receipts and expenses of the year. The estimates are accompanied by the " Plans for the Financial Administration of the Empire," which contain the basis of the estimates, specify the receipts and expenses more in detail, and explain deviations from previous years more precisely. In the German Empire the Reichstag and the Bundesrath, in Prussia the House of Deputies and the House of Peers, determine the Budget, and give it the force of law. The Reichstag and House of Deputies examine and authorise the raising and expending of the revenue for the German Empire and kingdom of Prussia respectively.

II. The discussion and authorisation of the financial laws are prepared, as a rule, by discussions in Committee. Each year a special Budget Committee is elected by the Reichstag and the House of Deputies, for preliminary discussion. This used to embrace all the estimates ; now this takes place, as a rule, only with those portions which, in the opinion of the House, require a specially sharp scrutiny. The Committee consists of 14 to 35 members. There are present at the discussions delegates from the Ministry of Finance, and from particular public departments, according to circumstances. At the close of the discussion the Committee decides on the proposals to be brought before the House, and appoints Reporters to furnish, either verbally or in writing, an account of the Committee's proceedings. If this strict form of discussion is not adopted, individual members of the House are appointed, by its President, as Commissioners for particular parts of the estimates, viz.: Schools, Forests, &c. The Government also nominates experienced officials as its own Commissioners for particular parts of the financial administration. The former get for the latter whatever information they require. These Commissioners often present long lists of questions, which are laid before the chiefs of the different departments, and are answered by them in writing. Questions and answers are printed, and distributed to the Members of the House.

III. Different Commissioners are appointed for different portions of the Financial Administration; but the Budget Committee is elected to examine the Budget as a whole. In Prussia it used to be the custom to divide the Committee into sub-committees, to which particular portions were referred for special discussion.

IV. The decisions of the Budget Committee constitute proposals, which are laid before the whole House, which adopts or rejects them after full discussion.

V. There are no special regulations with regard to the proceedings of the Budget Committee, as distinguished from the transactions of the Legislative Assemblies.

VI. It would seem that either a Committee is always appointed to examine the financial proposals of the year, or else Commissioners are nominated by the President of the House and by the Government respectively, the final decision resting with the Legislature.

VII. The answer to this question is best given in the concluding portion of Professor Nasse's letter, which follows.

Reply of PROFESSOR NASSE, *Professor of Political Economy.*

I. The Government, both of the German Empire and of the Prussian State, is obliged, before the commencement of every political year, to lay before the Reichstag or Landtag a detailed estimate of the whole receipts and expenses of the year. The estimates are accompanied by the "Plans

for the Financial Administration of the Empire," which contain the basis of the estimates, specify the receipts and expenses more in detail, and explain deviations from previous
years more precisely.

The determination of the particular receipts and expenses
which are likely to be involved in the administration in any
year, takes place before the beginning of the year, or in the
first months of it, in the form of a Law, which the different
factors of the Legislature must agree to. These factors are,
in the Empire, the Reichstag and Bundesrath ; in the
Prussian State, the House of Deputies, the House of Lords,
and the King. The estimates thus determined are published as a law, and form the legitimate standard for the
financial administration of the year in question.

The centre of gravity of the Parliamentary scrutiny of
the estimates is naturally found in the really representative
bodies—the Reichstag and House of Deputies—which every
year examine anew, and authorise each particular item in the
financial administration, and, in fact, determine both the
amount of the sums, and the purposes to which they are to
be exclusively applied. Here there is no distinction between
the expenses which are incurred on the ground of permanent
laws (*i.e.*, charges upon the consolidated fund), and those
applications of the revenue for which a permanent legal
foundation does not subsist.

II. The discussion and authorisation of the law in question
by the legislative assemblies is prepared for, as a rule, both
in the German Reichstag and the Prussian House of
Deputies by discussions in Committee. These are of two
kinds :—

First, There is elected, each year, by the Reichstag and
by the House of Deputies, a special Budget Committee for
preliminary discussion of the law. Until ten years ago, it
was the custom to refer all the estimates to the Committee
for preliminary discussion. At present, this takes place, as
a rule, only with those portions which, in the opinion of the
House, require a specially sharp scrutiny. At the discussions of the Committee, which consists of from fourteen to

thirty-five members, are present delegates from the Ministry of Finance, and also from the particular departments by which the expenses under discussion will be incurred, in order to give all necessary information, and defend the proposals of the Government. At the end of the discussions the Committee decides on the proposals to be brought before the House, and appoints one or more Reporters, who furnish reports of the transactions of the Committee, either verbally, or, in difficult and important questions, in writing. If this circumstantial and strict form of discussing the Budget is not adopted, individual members of the House are appointed by the President of the House as Commissioners for particular parts of the estimates (*i.e.*, for forests and domains, for schools, &c.). In a corresponding manner the Government also nominates individual high-grade officials, experienced in the subject, as its own Commissioners for particular portions of the financial administration. The former then draws from the latter all information that is necessary or appears desirable. They serve as instruments for this purpose, both for parties and individual members of the House. Frequently the Commissioners present long lists of questions, which are laid before the chiefs of the different departments, and answered by them in writing. Questions and answers are then printed, and handed to all members of the House.

III. At the appointment of the Commissioners, as already stated, different Commissioners are appointed for different portions of the financial administration ; the Budget Committee, on the other hand, is elected for the administration as a whole. Previously, however, it was the custom in Prussia, while the administration as a whole was discussed by the Budget Committee, to divide the Committee into sub-committees, to which particular portions were referred for special discussion.

IV. The decisions of the Budget Committee constitute proposals, which are laid before the whole house, and are adopted or thrown out after regular discussion.

V. and VI. There are no special regulations to guide the

discussions of the Committee, as distinguished from the other transactions of the legislative assemblies.

VII. When I compare the present condition with the time of absolute monarchical government before 1848, and contemplate the financial administration as a whole, I cannot avoid the conclusion, that there was greater economy in the expenditure, on the whole, in the first period. The absolute monarchy in Prussia was afraid to strain the taxation too much, and was especially careful to economise its resources. It was only in consequence of such excellent and highly economical administration that that form of Government could endure so long with us.

Now, no doubt in particular branches of the Administration the expenses are somewhat reduced through Parliamentary control, *e.g.*, in the military department, but in others they are actually increased, since the popular representatives themselves press for increased expenses on schools, on means of communication, &c. But, what is most important, the Government has no reason to dread, as before, the responsibility of increased expenditure. When the Government has once obtained the consent of the representative body, it is more sheltered than before against public opinion. The power of the State has been made stronger in this as in other spheres, through the introduction of popular representation.

Still, it would be a mistake to represent the Parliamentary control of the expenditure in Germany as ineffectual. It has, as mentioned already, influence over the *direction* of the public expenditure, and forms a guarantee against the encroachment of open abuses and gross extravagance in the administration of the revenues. Though previously even without much control the Prussian financial administration was excellent for a short time, yet the question may always arise, whether the old economy could be preserved under altered conditions, by which I mean greater prosperity of the whole people. There have been times in Prussian history, when in the absence of such control the public money has been squandered in an irresponsible manner; and

E

the yearly scrutiny and public discussion furnish a certain security against a recurrence of these really great abuses.

As regards economy of management in details and particulars, the popular legislature has really very little influence. Neither the time nor the information at the disposal of a parliamentary assembly are anything like sufficient to attain this object, even with the best division of their labours ; *e.g.*, such bodies cannot form any well-founded or independent judgment whether the officials make no unnecessary journeys, whether there is economical or wasteful management in the great workshops of the army, the navy, and the State railways. In this connection much is secured with us through the supervision of the "Chamber of Accounts," a free and independent board of professional officials, which has to conduct the control of the whole financial administration by examining and confirming the accounts of receipts, and outlay of the public money. It inquires whether the moneys voted to the Administration have been properly applied, and is excellently adapted for discovering instances of waste of the public money.

I will observe, lastly, that the great growth of the public expenditure in Germany may be regarded, partly at least, as a necessary result of two circumstances—first, our foreign political relations and the foundation of a united German Empire ; and, secondly, our increased prosperity, which has enlarged the public as well as the private requirements of the people. Just as more sugar, coffee, beer, is consumed per head of the population than thirty years ago, so we spend more on schools, art, and science, streets and roads, good buildings for the law courts, and other State offices, &c. In this relation the increase of the public expenditure is hardly to be regretted.

HOLLAND.

The following letter from M. J. L. de Bruyn Köps, member of the Lower House of the States General, gives a clear and succinct reply to the questions contained in the circulars sent by the Cobden Club.

The Hague, July, 1876.

Sir,—Referring to the questions of your circular I beg to state :—

I., III. At the beginning of each session in September the Government submits the proposed items of expenditure for the following year (1st January to 31st December) to the sanction of the Legislature, as required by the Constitution. The Budget is divided into chapters nearly corresponding with the Departments of the Administration or Ministries.

- *a.* Royal House.
- *b.* High Councils of State—viz., States General, Privy Council, Financial Board of Control.
- *c.* Foreign Affairs.
- *d.* Justice.
- *e.* Home Department.
- *f.* Navy.
- *g.* Finance, National Debt Department.
- *h.* War.
- *i.* Colonial.
- *j.* Unforeseen expenses.

An additional law specifies the ways and means for each year.

Each chapter forms a separate project of law, and is voted as such separately. The chapters are divided into articles for each item of expenditure. The articles are voted separately by the second Chamber, which has a right of amendment. The discussion in the Upper Chamber begins after the passing of the Budget by the Lower House, but the

Constitution gives no right of amendment to the Upper Chamber—it can only approve or reject, but can make no alteration.

A special Budget is proposed and discussed earlier in the year for the East India Colonies. It also is divided into chapters, discussed, and voted on in detail.

II., IV. The Budget is discussed in full Assembly, each article or item being voted separately. Before the public discussion each chapter is examined in the five sections or Committees (each consisting of sixteen members), into which the House is divided. Each section names a Reporter, the five Reporters form a "Commission for the Chapters of the Budget." They report, giving a full account of the observations made in the sections. The Report is printed, and communicated to the Government, which answers in a printed *mémoire*, thereby proposing such alteration as it deems fit.

V. Sections or Committees and Reporters have an independent action—the Reporters' Commission may add observations or proposals of their own, but this is not usually done in bills relating to expenditure.

VI. No expenditure can be made by Government if not distinctly sanctioned by Parliament. Each expenditure must be based on a special article of the Budget.

There is a totally independent board of control for finance, whose members are nominated for life by the second Chamber; its sanction is necessary for the payment of each item of expenditure. Heads of departments can make no order for payment unless it be revised and approved by this Board of Control.

The Board considers:

1. Whether the object of the proposed payment be in accordance with the articles of the Budget on which it is said to be founded.
2. Whether the credit of the particular article be exhausted, and whether it leaves sufficient funds disengaged

VII. The charges of administration have augmented generally both in civil and military branches.

	War.	Navy.	Total.
1852.	10,400,000	5,475,000	69,787,000 florins.
1876.	24,000,000	13,632,000	110,000,000 florins.

Still, the control of the Legislature may be said to work favourably. Items of new expenditure for new objects, or for the increase of old objects, are often rejected or amended, and the Government is careful to keep within the limits which the national representation desires.

It is to be observed that when the credit granted to a given article in the Budget is exhausted, the department under which that article comes can make a further expenditure, by means of the clause "unforeseen expenditure" attached to every chapter of the Budget, but only to a limited extent, about 50,000 florins upon an item of expenditure amounting to 15,000,000 or 20,000,000 florins. There is, besides, a final chapter for "unforeseen expenditure" for the use of the Government in general to the amount of 50,000 florins.

The part "unforeseen expenditure" in the various chapters can only be used for supplying insufficient articles specially designated in the Act of Parliament.

New objects of expenditure can only be met in some cases by charging them on the separate chapter of "unforeseen expenditure;" in other cases by legislative action.

Yrs., &c.,

(Signed)   J. L. DE BRUYN KÖPS.

To J. B. POTTER, Esq., M.P.

Letter from M. VISSERING.

Leiden, 11 *July,* 1876.

DEAR SIR,—I am happy to be able to give you some information concerning our financial administration in reply to the letter of 28th June, with which you favoured me. You will kindly excuse any incorrect expressions which may occur in these statements, in consequence of my want of practice in writing English.

Since the revision of our fundamental law in 1848 the regulations of the control of national expenditure work very satisfactorily. Before that date the Government had rather free hands in disposing of the public money; and the personal *régime* of our late King William I. (who abdicated in 1840) greatly abused this power. The principal object of the revision of our fundamental law was to check those abuses. At present the income and expenditure, not only of the mother country itself, but even of the Colonies, are under the strict control of. the States-General, and are checked as regards details by a special body called "Rekenkamer" (*cour des comptes*) which is wholly independent of the Government. Certainly, this control has not impeded a very large increase of yearly expenditure in the last twenty-five years, as the figures which I subjoin will show you. But this increase has taken place with the full assent of the States-General, sometimes even on their instigation. And the larger expenses are sufficiently met by constantly growing receipts from different sources, without increasing the burdens of the nation by new taxes.

I now proceed to offer you the following information upon the questions you put to me.

I. Every year, at the opening of the session of the States-General in September, the Government is bound to propose a complete and most detailed Budget of the income and expenditure of the ensuing year, to which is joined a survey of the sums received and paid out on the same heads in the two last years. Whenever in the course of a year any unforeseen wants arise, the Government has to propose in the same manner a special Budget containing the sums required, and the means to meet this extraordinary expenditure.

II. According to the rules laid down in the fundamental law, all Government Bills are delivered first to the second Chamber of the States-General. The members of this body divide themselves into five Special Committees or Sections for the preparatory examination of the Bill. Each of these Sections elects a Reporter, which charge is generally committed to a member of the Section who is reputed to be the most versed in the matter. The five Reporters collect and discuss the observations brought forward in each of the Sections upon the proposed Bill, and communicate with the Minister from whose Department the Bill has been issued, by a paper called *Voorloopig Verslag* (preparatory report). The Minister answers by a paper in which he maintains the provisions of his Bill against the remarks of the Sections, or modifies them in conformity with their observations. By this exchange of papers the subject is duly prepared for public discussion in the full House, where each member is qualified to expound his opinions and to propose his amendments. If the Bill passes (amended or not) in the second Chamber, it is forwarded to the first Chamber of the States-General, where it is examined in the same manner, first in the Sections, afterwards in the full House, with this exception only, that no more amendments can be proposed.

III. The fundamental law enacts that the proposed expenditure shall be divided into several heads or distinct Bills, representing the departments of the public service ; it further permits an extension of this division, so that the expenses of one department can be divided into several Bills.

At present the several Acts, containing together the whole of our national expenditure, are the following :—

1. An Act for the expenditure of the Crown.
2. „ for the expenditure of the great bodies of public service, called " High Colleges of State " (States-General, Council of State, &c.)
3. An Act for the Foreign Department.
4. „ „ Law Department.
5. „ „ Home Department.
6. „ „ Naval Department.
7a. „ „ National Debt.

7b.	„	„	Finance Department.
8	„	„	War Department.
9	„	„	Colonial Administration.
10	„	„	Allowances for unforeseen exigencies

(no more than £100,000 yearly).

Each of these heads has its own sub-divisions in chapters, paragraphs, and articles, with appointment of a maximum for every single article; and the members of the second Chamber discuss, and divide upon each article. The control of " the Rekenkamer " prevents the limits of the apppointed sum being ever exceeded.

IV., V., VI. No special answer is wanted. But it may be observed that the independent action of the " Reken-kamer " is secured by a law, which enacts that the members of this body are appointed for life by the Crown, out of a list of nominees presented by the Second Chamber of the States-General.

VII. Beyond any doubt these regulations have the effect of not only limiting, but of preventing, all abuses in our financial administrations. They have not, however, been able to keep down the charges of general expenditure, neither in the military and naval, nor in the civil services. From various causes this expenditure has continually increased, and is still growing. The only charges reduced are those of the national debt, by constant redemptions on a large scale since 1850—a redemption amounting now to nine millions of florins a year. But the necessity of providing the means of national defence has almost doubled the military and naval expenses. The fall in the value of money has obliged us to raise the salaries of all public officers. Extensive and most costly public works, such as railways, canals, docks, dykes, are undertaken and performed at the cost of nearly two hundred million florins since 1850, and the expenditure on the behalf of public schools is every year vastly growing.

I am, sir, yours respectfully,
S. VISSERING,
Professor at the University of Leiden.

To T. B. POTTER, Esq., M.P.

The following are the figures referred to in the introduction of this paper :—

RECEIPTS.

BUDGET OF THE STATE (*exclusive of receipts and expenditure in the Colonies*) FOR THE YEARS 1851 AND 1875.

ESTIMATES.	1851	1875
I. Taxes and Retributions	*Florins.*	*Florins.*
a. Direct taxes............	18,681,000	22,791,000
b. Excises	19,425,000	30,925,000
c. Customs...................	4,610,000	5,713,000
d. Stamps & Legacy Duty	9,108,000	17,457,000
e. Other taxes..............	1,370,000	4,891,000
II. Other receipts.............	17,596,000	25,000,000
	70,790,100	106,777,000

CHARGES.

	1851	1875
I. Expenses of the Crown	800,000	750,000
II. Colleges of State	591,000	599,000
III. Foreign Department...	519,000	606,000
IV. Law ,, ...	2,306,000	3,587,000
V. Home ,, ...	4,544,000	21,053,000
VI. Naval ,, ..	5,324,000	13,090,000
VIIA. National Debt	36,425,000	27,163,000
VIIB. Finance Department...	8,359,000	20,366,000
VIII. War ,, ...	10,558,000	18,503,000
IX. Colonial Office	118,000	1,203,000
X. Unforeseen expenses...	100,000	50,000
	69,644,000	106,970,000

12 florins = £1.

ITALY.

SUMMARY.

I. EACH year, within the first fortnight of March, the Minister of Finance must bring in his estimated Budget for the next financial year, beginning on 1st January and ending on 31st December. This Budget is divided into ten parts (or projects of law, as the Italians say), one refers to the income and nine to the expenditure; these correspond with the various ministries, and each part is divided into articles, so as to give the fullest possible details.

This proposed Budget must be approved by the two Chambers, receive the Royal assent, and be promulgated before the following January. Each one of the divisions of the Budget is divided into two chapters, one for the ordinary income and expenditure, and one for the extraordinary income and expenditure.

Each portion of the whole proposed Budget is preceded by a report, which shows the variations occurring from year to year.

Within the first fortnight of March, the Finance Minister lays also before Parliament the definite Budget of revenue and expenditure of the year just ended on the 31st December last. The whole is divided into the various items of revenue and expenditure, and a comparison is made between the estimated ways and means in the Budget, as proposed the year before, and the actual revenue and expenditure as realised in the Budget thus definitely laid before Parliament. At the same time the Finance Minister presents the actual condition of the Treasury resulting from the financial year terminated on the 31st December last.

II. The Chamber of Deputies elects at the beginning of the Session a general Budget Committee, composed of thirty members. This Committee examines both the proposed and the definite Budgets in all their details.

It can propose increase, decrease, or any alteration it sees fit, and reports accordingly to the House; so can every member of the House when the Budget is discussed there. The final decision rests with the House.

After the House has approved of the Budget, it goes before the Senate, which nominates a Finance Committee of fifteen members, to examine the financial proposals in all their details. The Senate then votes upon the proposals, having the same powers in the matter as the Lower House.

III. The General Budget Committee of the House is divided into sub-committees; each sub-committee examines the special part of the Budget assigned to it, and reports thereon. The final decision of the Budget Committee upon these various reports is presented in the form of a Report, laid before the House.

The permanent Committee of the Senate is not subdivided into sub-committees, but divides its work among each one of its fifteen members.

These Committees of the two Houses examine both the projected Budget of the year to come and the final or definitive Budget of the past year.

IV. Each Budget Committee draws its own conclusions, and reports to its own House. Each House decides finally on the proposals made to its members by the Committees and the Government. In case of disagreement between the two Houses, the matter in dispute is referred back to one or both of them, according to the circumstances of the case.

V. Each Budget Committee is, as has been said, appointed each by its own House—viz., the Chamber and the Senate. The Budget Committee has complete freedom of action, can examine the Ministers, and call for all necessary documents.

VI. No expenditure can be made outside the limits of the Budgets as passed by the Chambers. It is forbidden to make any transfer of expenditure from one head to another.

No payment can be made by the Treasury without the assent of the Court of Accounts (*corte dei conti*), whose members are completely independent of the Government, and irremovable. The Court would refuse its sanction to any expenditure not comprised in, or in excess of what had been approved under, the chapter or heading relating to such expenditure.

The Budget always contains a sum of £160,000 as a fund for meeting unforeseen expenses. There is also another sum of £160,000 as a reserve fund.

A catalogue of such expenses is laid down in the Budget law to which this reserve fund is applicable. When money is taken from this reserve fund, it is done by a royal decree upon the advice of a Council of Ministers. It must, however, be approved by the Court of Accounts, and be published in the official gazette of the kingdom. When Parliament re-assembles, the Government must bring in a Bill to authorise what has thus been done.

VII. There is no possibility of an excess of expenditure by the administration beyond what Parliament has sanctioned. Experience proves beyond doubt the utility of the Parliament's thorough examination of the Budget as a means of limiting expenditure, and of economising.

The action of the Court of Accounts (*Corte dei Conti*) in the practical administration of the finances is universally approved. The Government cannot spend a farthing beyond what Parliament has voted chapter by chapter, nor does it as a matter of fact exceed in the least degree the ways and means as voted by the two Houses.

The following detailed account of the Italian financial system was sent by Signor Minghetti, the President of the Council and Finance Minister of the last Italian Cabinet :—

I. Within the first fifteen days of the month of March, in each year, the Minister of Finance must present to Parliament the project of the proposed Budget (*il projetto di bilancio di prima previsione*) for the next financial year, which coincides with the solar year, 1st January to 31st December.

This Budget is presented with ten distinct projects of law, one of which is for the income and nine for the expendi-- ture, which correspond to the number of Departments. They are as follows :—

Finances.
Grace, Justice, and Public Worship.
Foreign Affairs.
Home Department.
Public Works.
War.
Marine.
Agriculture and Commerce.
Public Instruction.

These projected forecasts of the proposed Budget must be approved by the Parliament (Chamber of Deputies, Senate, and Sovereign) promulgated and published before 1st of January of the year to which they refer. Each one of these ten projected Budget Laws is divided into two heads (*titoli*)—first, Ordinary Income and Expenditure, and second, Extraordinary.

The Budget of the expenses of the Finance Ministry is divided into four parts, each one being again divided into the two heads just mentioned.

 a. Public Debt, Pensions (*dotazioni*), Guarantees.
 b. Expenses of Administration and State Monopolies.
 c. Ecclesiastical Patrimony.
 d. Reserve Fund.

Each head of the projected Budget is divided into a variety of items.

An idea of the proposals, and of the detailed examination of the Budget, may be gathered from the number of items

written in the Budget of 1875 for each Ministry. There are
212 items in the expenditure of the Finance Department;
40 in that of Grace and Justice; 16 in that of Foreign
Affairs; 103 in that of the Interior; 269 in that of Public
Works; 90 in that of Public Instruction; 45 in that of War;
51 in that of Marine; and 58 in that of Agriculture and
Commerce.

Most of these items are sub-divided into articles, so that
the projected Budget may be drawn out in the utmost detail.

Each one of the projects, which together form the Budget,
is preceded by an account made especially with the object
of showing the variations between one year and another.

One year after the presentation of the projected Budget,
as proposed in the first instance, that is to say in the first
fifteen days of March in the current year, the Minister of
Finance presents to Parliament, in the form of a single law,
the definite Budget of the past year, which includes both
revenue and expenditure.

In an appendix to the proposals, both of the projected
and definite Budget, are given the lists of the employés, any
changes that may occur, the statistical conditions, and the
explanatory notes which may be necessary.

The expenditure is divided according to each Ministry in
the definite Budget, but it is only divided into heads and
items.   The divisions of the sum belonging to each item
are given to each Ministry, which puts it in the form of a
decree, to be duly registered in the Court of Accounts.

In the definite or final Budget are made the additions and
rectifications of expenses belonging to each Ministry, including their respective debits and credits in preceding years,
with a project of the equalisation between income and expenditure, indicating at the same time the means proper to
attain that object.

Together with the project of the definite Budget the
Minister of Finance presents the state of the Treasury for
the financial year ended 31st December, from which results
an account of its actual and its past condition.

II. The Chamber of Deputies nominates, by ballot in

public sitting, at the beginning of each session, a General Committee for the balance of accounts, composed of thirty members.

The accounts must, by a fundamental law of the monarchy, be examined, discussed, and approved by the Chamber of Deputies before going up to the Senate.

The Senate, too, at the beginning of each session nominates in the same way a Permanent Finance Committee, composed of fifteen members. This Committee must examine the accounts and every other project of law which has direct relation to the State Finances.

The Committee of the Chamber of Deputies, like that of the Senate, may propose increase or diminution of expenses, or make any proposition it deems fit.

The discussion of the various accounts is carried on in both Houses in full assembly. Every deputy or senator has the right of proposing whatever he thinks proper.

The projected Budget (*di prima previsione*), must be voted in the months of November and December, and the law approving it is published before the 1st of the following January.

The definite Budget, as finally settled, is voted before the Parliamentary vacation in the months of May and June. The law approving it is at once printed and promulgated.

III. The General Committee nominated by the Chamber of Deputies elects its own president, two vice-presidents, and two secretaries. The Committee itself is further divided into sub-committees.

1. For the accounts of the Ministry of Finance.
2. For the accounts of the Ministries of Marine, Public Works, Agriculture, and Commerce.
3. For the accounts of the Ministries of the Interior and of Foreign Affairs.
4. For the accounts of the Ministry of War.
5. For the accounts of the Ministry of Grace and Justice, and of Public Instruction.

Each sub-committee nominates its president and secretary; it nominates also a special Reporter for each one of the ten accounts of the various departments. The Reports, first approved by the sub-committee, and then by the general committee, are in the name of this latter presented to the Chamber, printed, and distributed.

The permanent committee elected by the Senate nominates its own president, vice-president, and secretary. It is not divided into sub-committees, but distributes among its members the work of drawing up reports upon the various Budget projects.

The same Committees and sub-committees serve both on the projected Budget (*di prima previsione*) and also on the definite Budget (*di definitiva previsione*).

As regards this definite Budget, as finally proposed, a general Report upon the single project of law relating to it is drawn up and presented by the Minister of Finance, as well as a special Report on each single Budget.

The particular accounts of each Ministry form so many annexes to the definitive Budget.

IV. The Committees refer and propose matters directly to the Assembly or Chamber, which deliberates upon the proposals.

A reduction voted by the Chamber of Deputies may not be approved by the Senate, and on the other hand the Senate may vote a reduction not voted by the Chamber.

In this case the project of the Budget as amended, returns from the Senate to the Deputies. The report of the General Committee on the amendment passed by the other House is laid before the Chamber of Deputies, which discusses and votes according to the usual forms.

V. The Committees make their proposals to their respective Chambers, not to the Government. They possess the fullest independence, like the two Chambers by whom they are nominated. They have the right of examining the Ministers, and also of calling for documents, so as to obtain every kind of information.

VI. No expenditure can be made outside the limits of the Budget as approved by law.

It is forbidden to transfer expenditure from one item to another, either in the Budget as first proposed or as definitely arranged.

No order for payment can be carried out (*saldato*) by the Treasury without the sanction of the Court of Accounts (*corte dei conti*), composed of independent and irremovable magistrates, who refuse their assent when the nature of the expenditure does not correspond to the item to which it is assigned, or, if corresponding to it, it exceeds the sum assigned to the item. The definitive Budget having been verified, any new expense must be approved by a special law.

There is set down in the Budget a sum of £160,000 for unforeseen expenses. Another sum of £160,000 is inserted under the heading of Reserved Fund. In the Budget Law there is given each year a catalogue of these expenses, to meet which there is this reserved fund, when the sums inscribed in the respective chapters of the Budget are insufficient. In this catalogue are indicated the items for each Ministry; they have reference to the premiums for the collection of the various taxes.

The taking of a given sum from one of these two reserve funds is made by royal decree after due deliberation on the part of the Cabinet. The decree itself cannot be executed without bearing the registered assent of the Court of Accounts. It must also be published in the official gazette of the kingdom within ten days, and when Parliament re-assembles it must be presented to it to be converted into a law.

VII. No abuse from excess of expenditure is possible in the kingdom of Italy on the part of the Administration, as every expense must be first approved by Parliament, and the necessary funds be voted by it.

From the experience of many years no doubt remains as to the utility of the Parliamentary examination of the projected and definitive Budgets as a means of limiting expenses and producing economy, and consequently of lessening the burdens by which the public expenditure must be met. In the same way no one doubts the practical efficacy of the

F

control exercised by the Court of Accounts.   The Budget
is a serious matter.   The Government cannot spend a
farthing more than Parliament has allowed in each item of
expense.

The Government has neither the power nor the right to
go beyond the limits assigned by Parliament.

Signor Bodio forwarded from the Italian Ministry of Agriculture and Commerce the following replies to the questions
asked by the Cobden Club in its letter of June, 1876 :—

I. Within the first fifteen days of March the Minister of
Finance must present to Parliament (in printed form) the
project of his proposed Budget, both as regards revenue and
expenditure, relative to each of the nine Ministries for the
coming year.

These forecasts (*preventivi*) must be approved by law
before the 1st of January next following.

Within the first fifteen days of March the Minister of Finance
must present (in printed form) the definite Budget of the
year, to which it refers, with the rectifications and additions
of the expenditure, relating to the service of each Ministry,
together with the remains of the estimates of the past year,
and with a statement touching the balance between revenue
and expenditure.

Together with the definite Budget must be presented a
printed report of the state of the Treasury to the close of
the past financial year up to the end of December ; that is,
the condition of the Treasury, and the debit and credit
account of its management for the year.   The definite
Budget once approved, any new expense can only be approved by special law.

In the proposals presented to Parliament the means for
providing for new expenses must be indicated.

II. The Budget of revenue and expenditure must be discussed, and voted by the Chamber of Deputies, before going

to the Senate. The Chamber forms within itself a general Budget Committee, which is sub-divided into as many sub-committees as there are Budgets to examine, that is, one for the revenue and nine for the expenditure. The general Budget Committee is nominated by the Chamber of Deputies, by ballot. It is composed of at least thirty members, who are chosen for one year.

The permanent Finance Committee of the Senate answers to the general Budget Committee of the Chamber; however, this permanent Finance Committee is not only charged with examining the Budget, like the Committee nominated by the Chamber, but is also charged with the examination of all those laws which have a direct relation to the state finances. The Senatorial Committee is composed of 15 Members, and is not divided into sub-committees.

III. The general Budget of the State is divided into as many special Budgets as there are Ministries—that is, a Budget for the Ministry of Finance, Home Affairs or Interior, Foreign Affairs, Public Works, War, Marine, Public Instruction, Justice, Agriculture and Commerce. Each of these Budgets is examined and discussed by a special Committee ; these special Committees form the General Budget Committee.

IV. The Committees and sub-committees of the two Houses (Senate and Chamber of Deputies) can propose any modifications, but these can be adopted finally only by the Houses, which can accept, reject, or change them. The full accord of both Houses is necessary to every part of the Budget, in order that it, like every other law, may be presented to the Crown for its assent.

The answers given above are a sufficient reply to questions V. and VI.

VII. Before the present law concerning the state accounts came into vigour it often happened that the Government demanded of Parliament a bill of indemnity for expenses considerably beyond the funds approved by the Chambers.

Now, however, eventual and urgent expenses are provided for by appropriate provisions placed at the disposal of the Finance Minister ; one of these is called " Reserve Fund for Expenses Authorised and Obligatory" (*spese d'ordine ed obbligatorie*), and the other " Fund for Unforeseen Expenses." These provisions were made by the law of 22nd April, 1869.

For the year 1876 the whole sum allowed for these two funds was eight million francs, or four millions for each.

Reply from Sigr. Emilio Broglio, *Member of the Italian Chamber of Deputies.*

Piediluco, Terni, July, 1876.

Sir,—Properly speaking, it lies not precisely within my scope to furnish you with the information that you ask of the members of the Cobden Club in your circular of June, 1876.

There are among the members of the Cobden Club in Italy persons much more competent than myself, among others my friend Sigr. Marco Minghetti (who has more than once been for a considerable time Minister of Finance), who could reply consequently much better than I can to your questions.

However, I have not the right to be wholly silent, for various reasons. First, because, as Parliament is not sitting, I have not the means of informing myself whether my friend intends himself to reply to your questions ; secondly, because the system which you have, on this occasion, adopted of applying to the members of your Club, in order to obtain the information you desire, seems to me so just and natural that I am consequently forced to recognise the duty of reply on the part of those members to whom the questions have been addressed, more especially as on a former occasion I regretted to see you follow another method, whose consequences were (*fâcheuses*) unpleasant, as was the case when you received a letter from your countryman, Mr. Montgomery Stuart, on the supposed Protectionist tendencies (quite a wrong supposition) of Sigr. Minghetti's Government, which circumstance gave rise to very inexact conclusions (*appréciations*) in one of the last meetings of the Cobden Club ; thirdly, because, since you did me the honour of electing me as one of the members of the Cobden Club I have never been able to be of use to you, and I should feel some remorse if, now that I have the leisure for doing you a service, I should let slip the occasion without profiting by it.

The following are my replies to your questions. Our Government is obliged by law to present every year to Parliament, first to the Chamber of Deputies, the Budget law not later than the 15th March. Annexed to the Bill are the proposed items of expenditure for the current year, or, rather, for the following year, divided into the several heads, representing all the departments of the public service. These departments are nine in number. The Bill is sent for examination to a Select Committee of Ways and Means, composed of thirty members, elected by the Chamber at the beginning of each session, by the bad French method of bulletins—a somewhat complicated kind of ballot. The Select Committee is divided into sub-committees, for the investigation of the nine parts of the Budget. Each sub-committee, as soon as it has finished its examination, chooses a Reporter, who presents his Report first to the full Select Committee, where the Minister whose Budget is under consideration often appears to try and come to an agreement on the proposed economies. After discussion and approval in Committee, the Budget goes to the House. Then the debate opens there, first a general discussion, and then one on each of the items, which are finally voted one after another. The Court of Accounts refuses to countersign any order for payment which goes beyond the sum allotted.

I ought to say, by way of great exactness, that there are every year two Budget Bills, one in March, the projected

Budget (*de première prévision*), and one in November, the definite or final Budget; but this is a detail without importance, and which cannot last, because this double discussion entails an enormous expenditure of time and labour.

Much remains to be said. In the first place, as to the composition of the Select Committee. If the "Right" has the majority in the Chamber, that is the party at once liberal, wise, and moderate, the party of Count Cavour, which has governed the country since 1859 (except six months in 1862, which brought about the catastrophe of Aspromonte against Garibaldi, and six months in 1867, which brought about the catastrophe of Mentana, and again to-day after the vote of 18th March, 1876, which brought into power the actual Ministry of the "Left");—the "Right," I say, has always selected a committee naturally with a "Right" majority, but with a large representation of the "Left" so as to give it fair-play; to-day the "Left" is in power; that makes a difference. The result remains to be seen.

In conclusion comes your seventh question, which would require a book rather than a letter in reply. Generally speaking, it cannot be said that our Government presents neither abuses of administration nor excess of expenditure; the Minister of Finance, who is in general the Prime Minister, rigorously opposes such excess in the Cabinet, and, all things considered, with sufficient effect. In the House, sometimes, reforms and economies are made, but often the deputies from one locality or another, especially from the South, ask and obtain increase of expenditure for public works, roads, railways, ports, &c. &c.

What is needed is to divide, as in England, the Budget into two parts, one invariable, so long as a new law does not intervene to change it after careful examination, the other varying from year to year. With us, chiefly from following an unfortunate French initiative, the Budget bill is like any other, in which everything may be changed. Carlyle is not quite wrong (he is rarely quite right) when he says :— "Prussian Budget is fixed, many things are fixed. Why talk of them further? What pleasure there can be in having your household arrangements tumbled into disorder every new year by a new contrived scale of expenses I never could ascertain."

Yours, &c.

(Signed)   EMILIO BROGLIO.

Signor BOCCARDO *writes from Genoa in August,* 1876.

HONOURED SIR,—The following are a few observations which I am able to give in answer to your questions :—

I. Theoretically, in the Italian system of public accounts, the financial management can be easily known and discussed by the Legislature. The Government must in its proposed or projected Budget, and in its final one, enumerate each several head of expenditure proposed for the year.

II. Parliament examines and discusses each several head of expense in its Committees; a Committee is nominated for the Budget of each Ministry.

III. The proposed expenditure is divided into chapters representing the different departments of the public service, and each category of proposed expenses, with documents to elucidate them, is separately considered and studied by the Committees.

IV. The Committees refer their conclusions to Parliament, which discusses the proposals, and deliberates upon them.

It seems to me no particular replies are needed to numbers V., VI., and VII., because they are implied in those which precede.

(Signed)   GEROLAMO BOCCARDO.

T. B. POTTER, Esq., M.P.

PORTUGAL.

THE following letter from the Vicomte DE FIGANIÈRE gives a brief and clear statement of the mode in which the Portuguese Parliament deals with the Budget.

Cintra, Aug. 11th, 1876.

DEAR SIR,—In reply to your letter dated June 28th ultimo, requesting information with reference to the means adopted in Portugal for criticising and controlling the expenditure proposed by the Executive Government, and keeping in view the seven points in the order you have drawn them up, I have the honour to state :—

I. At the commencement of each session of the legislature the Minister of Finance presents the Budget containing the proposed items of expenditure for the current year.

II. Committees of the legislature are elected by the respective Houses (Deputies and Peers) to investigate the proposed items of expenditure. The Government Budget is divided into several heads, representing the principal departments of the public service (Home or Interior, and Public Instruction ; Finance ; Justice, and Ecclesiastical affairs ; Army, Navy, and Colonies ; Foreign Affairs ; Public Works, Commerce, and Agriculture). These divisions of the expenditure are referred for consideration to separate Committees. The latter take the time they think proper to consider the proposals submitted to them ; and when they deem it necessary they request the presence of the respective Crown Ministers in order to hear their reasons for any given proposal. The Committees then convert the " proposals " into " Projects of Law," either adopting or modifying the proposals (unless indeed they reject the " proposals " altogether), and finally present them to the House for discussion, accompanied with a report.

III. Answered under No. 2.

IV. The decisions of the said Committees in regard to any reduction of expenditure are subject to the revision of the Assembly, but not of the Government, whose only immediate action in the case at this stage is to take part in the discussion which follows in the House. I must add that, in practice, if the Government are earnest in maintaining their own proposals, and make it a "question of confidence" (of resigning in the event of failure), they generally carry their point if the majority which keeps them in power is sufficiently large.

V. There are no special arrangements made to secure the independent action of the Committees alluded to. Their independence depends, no doubt, upon the character of the House which elects them; if the latter should happen to be for the most part Governmental—*i.e.*, if the majority which support Ministers were overpowering—I take it that the independence of their Committees might very fairly be doubted.

VI. In view of what precedes, the answer under this head must be negative.

VII. This query also finds its answer indirectly in what has been already stated. In general I may say that, as far as my observation and recollection extend, the retrenchments which have been brought about occasionally in the public expenditure have mostly been the effect of proposals made by the Government themselves, of which I might quote some instances occurring within the last decade. But, to sum up, the character of the majority of the two Houses will of course always decide as to the real effective independence of the control of the Legislature in regard to expenditure. That this control has sometimes been found to be very effective and even troublesome is not to be doubted in view of what happened in the years 1867 to 1871, when two successive newly-elected Houses of Deputies refused to grant the additional taxes asked for by Ministers, and it was only after the fall of several Cabinets, rendered powerless by this action of the Legislature, and when the people really came to understand that unless they consented to part with a little more money it would be impossible to settle the financial embarrassments of the country—then only did they, the people, elect a Chamber of Deputies willing to sanction an increase of taxes.

Pray command me in whatever else I may be of use to the Committee of the Cobden Club, and

Believe me to be, dear sir,

Very faithfully yours,

FIGANIÈRE.

THOMAS BAYLEY POTTER, Esq., M.P.

RUSSIA.

Russia having no Parliament, and therefore no Parliamentary control of her expenditure, her method of dealing with her Budget is best explained by simply laying before the reader the two following statements. The first is drawn up by Lieut.-Gen. S. GREIG, Controller of the Empire ; and the second by M. BESOBROSOF, member of the Imperial Academy of Sciences, St. Petersburgh.

Statement drawn up by LIEUT.-GEN. S. GREIG, *Controller of the Empire, St. Petersburgh.*

In Russia the financial year corresponds with the calendar year, viz., it begins the 1st of January and ends the 31st of December.

The estimates of each Ministry are divided into paragraphs, which are subdivided into articles. A Minister has the power to move, in the course of the year, funds from one article to another of the same paragraph ; but he has no right to move funds from one paragraph to another. Should such a thing become necessary, he is obliged to ask a legislative vote empowering him to do so.

Each Ministry is obliged to prepare its estimates for a certain date, which, as well as the form of the estimates, is strictly regulated. The different estimates thus come to the Council of the Empire from August to October, and the dates of their presentation are so arranged that the estimates of the smaller departments are examined first, and those of the larger and more complicated, such as War, Marine, Public Works, Domains, come at the end.

The Council of the Empire, the supreme political body of

the realm, is the Legislative Assembly of Russia, and is composed of members appointed for life by the Emperor.

It is divided into permanent Committees or departments, one of which, the department of State " Economy," examines all the bills regarding finances and trade. It is before this department that the estimates are laid. At the same time each Ministry is obliged to communicate a certain number of printed copies of its estimates to the Minister of Finance and to the Controller of the Empire. In the Treasury, as well as in the Control Department, these estimates are examined with the greatest care and in the most minute details; and memoranda containing critical observations, proposals of reductions and other suggestions, are communicated by them to the Department of Economy. The Minister whose estimates these observations concern, takes knowledge of them, and is allowed a week to answer them.

The department then proceeds to the examination of the estimates, in the presence of the Controller of the Empire. Each "paragraph" and "article," both of revenue and expenditure, is examined separately, and the department draws up a resolution, either approving the ministerial demand or altering it. If an understanding is not come to with the Minister, the question is brought before the " Plenum," or general Assembly of the Council, and decided there by vote. This, however, happens seldom, and questions of detail are almost always settled in the department of Economy.

Every member of the Council of the Empire receives a printed copy of all the estimates, and of the observations thereon made by the Minister of Finance and by the Controller, as well as of the "journals" of the department of Economy, in which its votes on each item are consigned. Members may send to the department of Economy their remarks on any of the estimates, but few avail themselves of this right.

When all the estimates of revenue and expenditure have been settled by mutual agreement of the department of Economy with the Minister of Finance and the Controller, the Minister of Finance draws up the State Budget, which is a summary of items of the principal heads.

The Budget is discussed in the general assembly of the Council of the Empire on a special day about the middle of December. Together with it are placed on the orders of the day the Budget account for the preceding year of the Controller, and the cash account of the Minister of Finance. In practice, the discussion in the general assembly has scarcely ever an *immediate* effect on the figures of the Budget. And, in truth, after the long and laborious task of the department of Economy, there is hardly room for improvement. However, the discussion in the " Plenum " is neither without interest nor use. Criticism is heard, suggestions are made, which in some form or other appear embodied in next year's Budget, or in some useful measure or law. Doubts are cleared up, erroneous information rectified, imperfect knowledge instructed, the financial policy, in whole or in parts, attacked and vindicated.

When the Budget is voted by the general assembly of the Council, it is submitted by the Minister of Finance to the Imperial sanction, and then becomes law.

The proceedings of the Council of the Empire are perfectly free and independent, and there has been no example of its discussions being fettered or its votes disregarded. It is customary, however, that no member takes the initiative of a proposal which may lead to an augmentation of expenditure ; but this custom is certainly a good and safe one.

The supervision of the way the revenue is collected, and public money spent, is vested in a special institution called the Control of the Empire. The Control does not form part of the Treasury, as the Audit Office in England ; it is not shaped as a court of law, as the *Cour des Comptes*, in France. It is a special Ministry, organised on the pattern of other Ministries in Russia, having for its head a Cabinet Minister, who is called Controller of the Empire. As a rule, every province or government, as they are termed, has a Chamber of Control, of which there are sixty in Russia. These Chambers are quite independent of the Governors, general-governors, or any local administrator, being under the direct authority of the Controller of the Empire. The provincial and district treasuries, as well as the special receiving offices, are bound to send all documents on which they have either paid or received money, to the Chamber of Control, to which they are accountable. The Control Chambers have, moreover, the right to ask for any papers or correspondence they find necessary to examine, from any Government office within their province. To their control is subject not only the manipulation of moneys, but of materials, such as stores, ammunition, clothing, Crown works, arsenals, mines, &c. It is their duty also to make unexpected revisions of treasuries, and special receiving offices. They have the right of inspecting custom-houses, post-offices, and so on. In the audit of documents they have to look not only that taxes are properly collected, and money and materials lawfully spent, but they are bound to go into details of management, and examine whether contracts have been properly and judiciously entered into; whether Crown lands, forests, mines, &c., are not improperly managed; whether custom, excise, and other duties come in full due, and so on. When an unlawful expenditure or a drawback in revenue is ascertained, the Chamber claims back the money. If the delinquent does not submit, the case goes before the Council of the Control, presided over by the Controller of the Empire, and in some instances before the Senate.

The Ministers and Ministerial departments · are not accountable to the provincial Chambers. Expenditure made under their direct orders is revised by the central departments of the Control in St. Petersburgh, but otherwise the procedure is as stated above. The Control exists since the reign of the Emperor Alexander I.; but it has been completely reorganised in the present reign. The work of reform was carried through by the Secretary of State, Tatarinoff, late Controller of the Empire, who was chosen for and warmly supported in this very difficult task by the Emperor.

The great difference between the old and the new system is

that before this in Russia, and up to the present time in most
of the countries of Europe, the corresponding institutions (Audit Office, *Cour des Comptes, Rechnungs-kammer*, &c.), audited
accounts made up by the spending departments, while the new
Control does not audit the accounts, but the money documents.
In this way it controls the expenditure as soon as it is incurred,
and cannot be baffled by false or ingenious accounts, because
it examines no accounts, but prepares them itself from the
original money documents, these last reaching it automatically,
so to say, and as soon as money is paid out by the Treasury.
The accounts drawn up by the Control are published, and
justly entitled to the consideration of being perfectly trust-
worthy. They are of necessity very voluminous, but the
explanatory memorandum of the Controller of the Empire,
of which a French translation is subjoined, is sufficient for
practical purposes. It has been said that it comes out too late.
But it must be borne in mind that many items of credit or of
expenditure are allowed in Russia to run on for three months
after the general closing of the Budget. (It is contemplated
to do away with this curiously-termed "privileged period").
Then Russia is an immense country. There are upwards of
six hundred provincial and district treasuries, besides more
than three thousand "special receivers" (custom houses,
post and telegraph offices, courts of law, and justices of
peace). And it takes time to get accounts from the Chambers
of Control in the Caucasus, Turkestan, Western and Eastern
Siberia, with the Amour province bordering on the Pacific,
or even Archangel. Then all that mass of accounts must be
distributed under the different heads of revenue and expenditure, and got through all the stages of printing (think what
printing and correcting a volume of ciphers is!) With all
this the accounts for, say, 1874, have been presented to the
Council of the Empire on the 1st of October, 1875, and the
explanatory memorandum of the Controller been ready a
month after.

Besides this report on the accounts to the Council of the
Empire, the Controller delivers annually into the hands of
the Emperor a special report, in which he makes a review

of the principal heads of revenue and expenditure for the preceding year, stating in particular such cases of abuse, mal-administration, or mismanagement, discovered by the Control of the Empire, which specially deserve the attention of the sovereign. The autograph annotations and resolutions of his Imperial Majesty on this document act as a very powerful, nay, the most powerful, engine for promoting order, economy, and honesty in the administration of public money.

Now comes the last and most difficult question : " Has it been found that the course pursued has had the effect of keeping down the expenditure, or of limiting abuses connected with its administration ? " It is a difficult question, because, in all justice, the answer cannot but be affirmative, and yet figures cannot be adduced to prove it. On the contrary. The expenditure of the country has been rapidly increasing. To take only the last five years for which we have audited the accounts, we find that in 1874 the expenditure has risen, in comparison with 1870, by $11\frac{3}{4}$ per cent. The increase is due to different causes. Prices have gone up considerably, the railways having had the effect of raising them in places of produce, without effecting, at the same time, a corresponding fall in places of consumption. A great number of schools and colleges have been added to the existing ones. New Tribunals of Justice, much more costly, but incomparably better, than the old ones, have been created. Thus, in the last five years, the estimates of the Ministry of Public Instruction have risen by 30 per cent., and those of Justice by 20 per cent.

But, then, during the same period, the revenue has increased by sixteen per cent., though the taxation has not been raised, the impost on spirits excepted. The other taxes and imposts being remodelled, have been rather lowered, with the view of making them capable of yielding more revenue. Besides, the supplementary credits have gone down remarkably ; from 35,800,000 roubles in 1870 they have gradually fallen to 23,700,000 roubles in 1874. And from a long period of deficits, Russia has come to possess in her treasuries a sum of fifteen millions of roubles, which represent the surplus of revenue over expenditure for these last years.

Such a result certainly is due in a great measure to the severity with which the estimates and supplementary credits are scrutinised in the department of State Economy, in the Treasury, and in the Control. Though expenditure is still on the increase—such, by-the-by, being the case also in almost all the rest of the world—there is no doubt it would have increased much more if those agencies had not been at work—and at hard work—to keep it down. Not only less money is voted than asked for, but less is asked, because people, when they come to know how extremely difficult and bothering it is to get money, abstain more and more from asking for it. And as to the way money is spent after it has been voted, there are evident signs of more thrift. The Control is watchful and severe, and people do not like to get into a scrape with it. Money unduly spent, though it be through misunderstanding, must be returned with fines, sometimes heavy, and in cases of abuse or malversation, the delinquent is dragged before the criminal courts. All this tends to make heads of departments more watchful and careful, and the subordinate officials more orderly and honest.

It may be added that to keep down the expenditure a special and peculiar measure has been adopted some three years ago, on the proposal of the Minister of Finance. The war and marine estimates have been limited by a fixed sum for five years, it being forbidden to exceed this sum in annual estimates and supplementary credits put together. In this way the Treasury is safe, for a given period, from an increase of expenditure in the two largest spending departments of the State.

Statement drawn up by M. BESOBROSOF, *of the Imperial Academy of Sciences, St. Petersburgh.*

As there is no representative assembly in Russia, the Council of the Empire, composed of members quite in-

G

dependent of the administration, performs the functions of the supreme legislature. The proceedings in the Council of the Empire are almost the same as those in the representative bodies of constitutional countries.

The Budget is presented each year to the Council of the Empire, and discussed by it in all details both of revenue and expenditure. With this object each separate Budget, for each department, and for each particular administration, is sent to the Minister of Finance, and is presented by him, with his criticisms, to the Council of the Empire in September.

In each one of these Budgets the smallest details of revenue received by the various departments, and the credits which are allowed them, are noted down. A peculiarity in the Russian procedure is the criticism on the Budget presented to the Council of the Empire by the Controller of the Empire, at the same time as the statement of the Finance Minister. The Controller has the same rank as a Minister of State. He and the Finance Minister work together on the Budget before it is discussed in the Council of the Empire, and they communicate to it their several views, which are not always in agreement with each other. The Finance Committee of the Council of the Empire discusses each departmental Budget in the presence of the Finance Minister, of the Controller, and, when necessary, of the chief of the department whose special Budget is under consideration. After prolonged deliberations, the Ministry of Finance draws up the general Budget of the Empire, which is discussed in the Finance Committee of the Council of the Empire, and then presented to its full assembly (or Plenum) at the end of the year, with all the additions and special Budgets of each department. Then the Budget, with all its details fully drawn out, is published by the Senate in the collection of laws (*le recueil des lois*) at the beginning of each year. All this procedure is very long, and occupies very seriously and completely the Council of the Empire and the various Ministries; the heads of departments are often called before the Council to discuss the minutest details. Before the publication of the Budget, it is ratified by the Emperor, like all the laws emanating from the Council of the Empire.

If there is any very special matter (such as a deficit) in the Budget, it is further discussed in a special private Committee, under the Chairmanship of the President of the Council of the Empire, and some of the great dignitaries of State ; this Committee is not a public body, and its debates are secret.

According to law the Budget must be discussed in all its parts in the general assembly (or Plenum) of the Council of the Empire, but it is never done in practice, and the Budget is usually accepted as a whole by the assembly, because all the details are revised by the Finance Committee of the Council. Various members make general observations and speeches, but the procedure of the Plenum is brief.

In the Finance Committee of the Council each chapter and each paragraph of the Budget is discussed separately with the greatest attention. There is often much disputing with the chiefs of the different departments, and each little detail is thoroughly gone into.

The Plenum or General Assembly of the Council have the right, as has been already said, to revise the opinions expressed by the Finance Committee, but it is rarely done. Everything is done in the Committee (which is composed of five or six members), in the presence of the Finance Minister and of the Controller of the Empire.

The Finance Committee of the Council of the Empire is by law and in fact quite independent of the Administration, whether of the finance department or of any other Ministry. The Committee often materially changes the Budget, and, if necessary, reduces the expenses. Naturally, the opinion of the Finance Minister (who, like all the other Ministers, is a member of the Council of the Empire) has very great weight, but is not decisive (*définitive*). To prevent coming before the General Assembly with a diversity of opinions, some compromise is usually come to between the Ministers and the Finance Committee.

In Russia the national expenditure increases every year,
but as the revenue has increased in a yet greater proportion
during the last few years, the increase is not a cause of
alarm.   However, reasonable reductions of expenditure
should be made in Russia as in other countries.   The
defect in the Russian procedure, as it seems to me, is that
the Government (the Council of the Empire) attaches more
importance to the details than to the general complexion of
the Budget.   Considerable reductions are made of the
roubles and the copecks, but a reduction of millions could
be effected if the general character of the Budget were
seriously discussed.   Perhaps the cause of this is the absence
of the representative element in the Government.

(Signed)   、 W. BESOBROSOF.

SWEDEN.

The following reply was sent, just in time for publication (May, 1877), by M. OLOF WIJK, *a Member of the Swedish Parliament.*

I. According to the Constitution, the Ministers of the Crown have at the opening of each ordinary Riksdag to deliver two copies, one to each House, of the propositions relative to the condition of the Treasury and its requirements for the coming year (reckoning from the next 1st January to the 31st December following), together with the proposals as to how the necessary means are to be obtained.

These expenses are arranged under nine heads, including.

> Civil List.
> Justice.
> Foreign Affairs.
> Army.
> Navy.
> Civil Administration (Railways, &c.).
> Finance (Revenue Department).
> Ecclesiastical Affairs (Education, Science, &c.).
> Pensions.

And these heads are divided into detailed separate grants.

Proposals with regard to public expenses, which are not included in the Government proposals, may at any time be brought forward by Ministers during the sitting of the Riksdag.

Every proposition of the Government must be accompanied by the reasons for the same given by the chief of the respective department before His Majesty in Council.

The Crown thus has the initiative in the matter of the
Budget, but the Riksdag also has a similar right which can
be exercised in case a member of either Chamber proposes
a grant, which, however, by rule, must be done within ten
days from the opening of the Riksdag.

II. No proposal of the Government for a grant, nor of any
individual member of the Riksdag can be taken into consideration by the Chambers, and decided before the " Stats
Utskottet " (select Committee of Finance) has given its
opinion on the subject. This Committee is composed of
twenty-four members, half of whom are appointed by each
Chamber from among its own members. When the Committee, which has access to all the Government accounts and
journals, has gone through the proposals made, it has to
deliver to the Chambers its judgment in the matter, together
with the grounds on which such judgment is favourable or
unfavourable to the proposals of the Government, or of
individual members ; or changes may be recommended in
any such proposition. In these judgments the various items
entering into each grant are considered separately in detail.

III. The division of the expenses is already indicated in
the proposals of His Majesty's Government under the nine
separate heads already given ; all expenses are considered
together by the same select Committee of Finance. In
order to spare time, and insure the proper order of
business, the Committee, as it proceeds in its work of
examination, communicates to the Chambers its judgment
of each separate head. Towards the end of the session,
however, the Committee makes up, and communicates to the
Chambers for general consideration, the so-called " Finans
Betankandet," or proposal of ways and means, including all
the State requirements, grounded upon the definitive resolutions adopted by the Riksdag during its discussions of
the Budget.

IV. In questions of public expenses the Committee has
no right of decision, but only of inquiry. The propositions, whether of the Government or of individual
members of the Riksdag, come back from the Committee

to the Chambers, accompanied by the former's remarks. The proposals are then, at the same time, laid before the House, and the Chambers come to a definitive decision, either affirmative or negative, relative to each separate item, as it is brought forward, with such statements as are recommended by the Committee or proposed by any individual member during the discussion. Members of the Government have the right of defending their propositions in the Chambers, and of opposing alterations in them, but the determination of the public expenditure belongs exclusively to the Riksdag, with the restriction that reductions of already existing grants to public institutions, when such reductions would render impossible the continued action of such public bodies, are dependent upon his Majesty's consent.

What the two Chambers agree upon determines the decision of the Riksdag. But if, in the matter of any grant, the two Chambers arrive at opposite conclusions, and cannot, by any proposal of the Committee, be brought to agree, then each Chamber votes separately on the question in dispute. The votes in both Chambers are then added together, and the plurality of votes thus taken gives the decision of the Riksdag. To provide against the case of equal numbers in a voting of this kind, one vote is delivered and sealed up in the lower Chamber, which, in case of an equal number of votes being given, is opened, and so the question is decided.

Inasmuch as the second Chamber is more numerous than the first (at the present moment 198 members to 134), the Constitution has thus, in questions of finance (in which the Chambers disagree, and recourse is had to the above mode of voting together), given to the lower Chamber a greater influence. This is the only advantage that it enjoys in questions relating to the Budget. In the Chambers all the votes are secret.

V. The Government has no influence in the appointment of the Committee, neither have its members access to the Committee's meetings. The Committee is appointed exclusively by the Chambers, and is thus usually an expression of the views of the majority in the Chambers.   It must be remembered that the Committee has no right of decision, but only of inquiry.   The right of decision belongs exclusively to the two Chambers, which have equal rights, and discuss separately and simultaneously the public expenditure.

VI. Answered in the foregoing paragraphs.

VII. Reason for complaint of abuse in the management of the sums voted for the expenditure is hardly to be found. Besides the ordinary arithmetical control, there is indeed a further control in the right possessed by the Committee to examine not only the proposed Budget but also the accounts of the administration in preceding years, with the assistance of a previous revision, made by twelve Revisors, nominated for that purpose at every Riksdag, by the Chambers, each Chamber appointing half the number.   The power of the Riksdag to resist the Government's demands for grants, appears, in fact, to be fully established.   The proposed Budget does not, in general, pass the Chambers without being subjected to greater or less modifications. That the increasing public expenditure has hitherto always been met by an increasing public income, in spite of the reduction of many very unequal and oppressive taxes, is a consequence of the rapid development, both intellectual and material, of the country.

Stockholm, May, 1877.   (Signed)   OLAF WIJK.

UNITED STATES.

SUMMARY.

I. At the beginning of each session, in December, the proposed expenditure for the next fiscal year, of the different departments of the Federal Government, is submitted to Congress in full detail.

II. To a standing Committee, known as the Committee on Appropriations, in the House of Representatives, these several estimates are submitted. In the Senate they are referred to the Committee on Finance. Each House of Congress appoints also other Committees, to supervise the expenditure of different departments of the government : as the Committee on Foreign Affairs, Judiciary, Military, Naval, &c. Special Committees are charged to review the expenditure which has been incurred by the several executive departments. The bills authorising expenditure are in the first instance reported to the House of Representatives by the Committee on Appropriations, and to the Senate by the Committee on Finance.

III. It is the practice to divide the proposed expenditure into several heads answering to the various public departments. The Committee of Appropriations, and the Finance Committee, respectively belonging to the House of Representatives and to the Senate, investigate proposed expenditure in detail, confer with the heads of the several departments, and have power to summon witnesses when it is deemed expedient to do so.

IV. The decisions of the committees are reported to Congress, which debates and votes upon them, both as to details and as to the whole expenditure. The concurrent action of the two Houses is necessary before any Bill is submitted for approval to the Executive. This latter has a right of veto, which is exercised by sending back the Bill to the House in which it originated, with reasons for so doing. But a two-thirds majority in each House can pass any Bill over the veto of the President of the United States.

V. The Committees intrusted with the supervision of appropriations and expenditure act independently, and are alone responsible to that branch of the legislature from which they emanate.

VI. The law forbids any department of state from incurring expenditure other than that which is authorised by law.

VII. The tendency in the United States is to increasing expenditure, owing especially to the war of 1861 to 1865. Investigations by Congress and public discussions have a a counter tendency.

———————

Statement drawn up by the Hon. HENRY L. DAWES, *Senator for Massachusetts, and previously Chairman of Committee of Appropriations in the House of Representatives. (Forwarded by* Mr. GEORGE WALKER.)

I. The Secretary of the Treasury is required by law to submit to Congress at the commencement of each regular session (first Monday in December) the estimates of each Bureau in each department for the current expenses of those Bureaux for the fiscal year commencing July 1st next following. Extraordinary and unusual expenses are estimated for as the exigency arises.

II. These estimates are referred to a Committee on Appropriations in each House, to report the necessary Bills for the action of their respective Houses. These Bills originate usually, not necessarily, in the House of Representatives. It is the ambition of the Committee of Appropriations in preparation of the Bills to cut down each item of the estimates to the lowest possible point. They are then reported to the House, and by it referred to the Committee of the whole House for discussion and amendment.

III. The estimates, and the Bills prepared upon them, are reduced to the minutest details of items the nature of the case will admit of. These subdivisions are not usually referred to any other Committees, but are considered in Committee of the whole.

IV. The decision of the Committee of Appropriations is only recommendatory, and their Bills are subject to any amendment, either in Committee of the whole, or in the House after them, as a majority shall determine. In practice, almost every item is contested, some one member playing the *rôle* of economist, and leading the attacks. The " Government," *i.e.*, the Executive branch, must take them as they finally pass both Houses.

V. The Committees on Appropriations, like all other standing Committees, are appointed in the House by the Speaker, and in the Senate by the election of the body, and therefore always have a majority of the political character of the body in which they act. In the present Congress that majority is one way in the House and the other way in the Senate.

VI. In practice Congress has no other method.

VII. In practice the tendency has been, on the part of the estimates—*i.e.,* the Executive branch—to an increase, and on the part of the legislature to a decrease. It used to be said that the Bureaux, expecting to be cut down by the legislature, would estimate above their necessities for a margin. The average annual reduction of ordinary expenditures under the present Administration (since March 4, 1869) has been about 9,000,000 dols.

Reply of Mr. L. F. S. FOSTER *and* Mr. DAVID A. WELLS.

Norwich, Connecticut, U.S., July 24*th*, 1876.

DEAR SIR,—Each of us have received a copy of the Cobden Club circular of June 28, 1876, asking information respecting the means adopted in the United States for criticising and controlling the expenditures proposed by the executive

department of the Government.   We unite in submitting
the following statements, in answer to the several questions
proposed :—

I. The several departments ot the Federal Government
submit to Congress, at the commencement of each session,
the proposed amounts of expenditure for the next fiscal
year, with the various items, in detail.

II. These several estimates are referred, in the House of
Representatives, to a standing committee, known as the
Committee on Appropriations, and in the Senate to a committee known as the Committee on Finance.   There are
also, in each House of Congress, other committees, entrusted
with the supervision of the several departments of the
Government, as the Committee on Foreign Affairs, Judiciary,
Military Affairs, Naval Affairs, Pensions, &c., as well as
special committees, charged with the duty of reviewing the
expenditures which have been incurred by the several
executive departments.   All these take cognisance of the
proposed expenditure, but the Bills authorising the expenditures are primarily reported for action, in the House of
Representatives by the Committee on Appropriations, and
in the Senate by the Committee on Finance.   These two
committees investigate in detail, confer with the heads of
the several departments of the Government, and have
power to summon such witnesses as they may deem expedient.

III. Answered in Nos. I. and II.

IV. The decisions of the several committees in reference
to expenditure having been reported respectively to the two
Houses of Congress, they are then made the subject of
careful examination and debate in open legislative session,
a vote being taken, when demanded, on the several items,
and finally on the Bill as a whole, revised and amended.
The concurrent action of the two Houses is requisite before
any Bill is submitted to the executive for approval.   The
executive has a right to veto, which is done by sending the
Bill back to the House in which it originated, with the
executive's reasons for not signing it.   Congress, by two-thirds
majority in each House, may pass any Bill over a veto.

V. The Committee of both Houses, entrusted with the supervision of appropriations and expenditures, act independently of each other, and are responsible only to the branches of Congress of which they form a part.

VI. It is forbidden by law for any department of Government to incur any expenditure other than those which are authorised by law, but these provisions are almost always, in greater or less degree, evaded, and "deficiency bills" form a part, almost invariably, of the Appropriation Acts of each session.

VII. The tendency of every department of the Government of the United States, the two Houses of Congress not excepted, is to continually increase expenditures, and this increase, since 1861, owing especially to the war, has been very great. Investigations by Congress, and discussions by the public, have a counter tendency to repress expenditures and promote economy; but increasing expenditure is the crying evil at present in every department of Government in the United States, State as well as Federal. In short, everything tends to cheapen in the United States except the Government.

In our opinion there can be, under a Republican form of Government, no so efficient check on Governmental expenditures as earnest and intelligent public sentiment in favour of economy. When the people are indifferent, waste and extravagance will be the rule, frugality and wise discretion in expenditures the exception.

We are, very respectfully,

Your obedient servants,

L. F. S. FOSTER.

To T. B. POTTER, Esq., M.P.   DAVID A. WELLS.

Reply of MR. CLARKSON N. POTTER, *of New York.*

The answers below relate to the Congress of the United States, where all Appropriation Bills must originate in the

House of Representatives, but can be amended—*i.e.*, increased or diminished—in the Senate, in which amendments the House must concur. In this respect, and also in the the practice of making appropriations, the action of the State legislatures generally substantially conforms to that of Congress.

I. Yes.

II. Bills appropriating money must be first considered in the Committee of Appropriations (eleven members), which report the Appropriation Bills in a form they approve to the House, where they are considered in Committee of the whole House, and, as settled in that Committee of the whole House, recommended to the House. Certain subjects—like the expenditures of the post office department, and expenditures for improving rivers and harbours, &c.—are first considered in Committees having those subjects specially in charge. Their action is then referred to the Committee on Appropriations. In other cases the Committee on Appropriations acts directly.

III. Yes, as stated in No. II.

IV. Yes, to revision by the Assembly. If by the Government is meant the Executive, No. The Executive has no control whatever over the legislation for expenditures, except that all the Bills require the President's assent, and if that be refused the Bill can then only be adopted by a vote of two-thirds of each House.

V. They are permanent Committees upon particular subjects, and must report to the House.

VI. The Executive can spend nothing for which the legislature has not first made appropriation.

VII. Yes, in a degree.

Reply of Mr. J. S. Moore, *Editor of the " New York World."*

New York, July 12th, 1876.

Sir,—I have the honour to acknowledge your printed communication, dated 28th June, requesting information with reference to the means adopted in the United States for criticising and controlling the expenditures proposed by the Executive Government.

Your communication contains seven questions, to which you require specific answers. I have much pleasure in giving the honourable committee of the Cobden Club as full an explanation as my observation on the subject can furnish.

I. The procedure is as follows, viz. : Congress is by law required to meet on the first Monday in December. During that month when the House is in session, the Secretary of the Treasury transmits the estimates of appropriations for the following fiscal year, required for the whole service, in the shape of a letter addressed to the Speaker of the House.

I send by this mail a cópy of such a letter of estimates for the year 1874, which will give you some idea of the procedure.

But to make it as plain as possible, I will only add that the following Departments, viz :

Civil Establishment—Treasury Department.

Foreign Intercourse—State Department.

Military Establishment—War Department.

Naval Establishment—Navy Department.

Indian Affairs—Interior Department.

Pensions—Interior Department.

Public Works—War, Navy, Interior, and Treasury Departments.

Postal Services—Post Office Department.

Miscellaneous—Treasury Department.

Permanent Appropriations—Treasury Deparment ;
each transmitted to the Secretary of the Treasury estimates for the requirements of their respective departments for the next fiscal year, commencing on the 1st of July.

The Secretary to the Treasury then has these estimates printed in the form I send them, and sends it to the Speaker of the House always, if possible, during the first week of the session.

II. In order to answer this question it is necessary to state that all Legislation in the Federal Congress is first submitted to the appropriate Committees, a list of which I hereby transmit.

Thus, then, the Secretary's estimates are given out by the Speaker of the House to the Committee created for that special purpose, viz., the Appropriation Committee. That Committee then goes carefully through the Secretary's estimates, in order to lay before the House their own revised estimates for the service. It is their duty and privilege to reduce or add, as they find it necessary to the Secretary's estimates, and very frequently large sums are added by the Appropriation Committee for services, buildings, public works, and many other things which are not found in the Secretary's estimates.

III. The Committee of Appropriation divides the estimates into several bills; for instance, the Foreign Intercourse is a separate bill, Postal Service is another, Indians, Pensions, &c., &c. Each of these separate bills, after being perfected in the Appropriation Committee, is given in charge of one of the members of that Committee, whose duty it is to present it to the Committee of the whole House. The member having such a bill in charge moves for the Speaker to leave the chair, and for the House to resolve itself into a Committee of the whole House. The Speaker then appoints a chairman, and leaves the chair. The Bill then is brought before the Committee of the whole House, debated and discussed, and amendments are in order, which are voted on by tellers, and not by "yeas" and "nays."

The Bill, then, thus amended, is passed through this Committee of the whole, and is immediately brought before the House—that is to say, the Committee rises, and the Chairman reports to the Speaker the passage of the Bill in Committee. The Speaker then puts the question from the chair whether the Bill shall pass, and the passage of the Bill is subject to the ayes and nays—that is, for members to record their names for or against the measure ; but the Bill at that stage is no longer debatable.

IV. Of course, as I already explained, any member may move an amendment, and give his reason ; and very often estimates made by the Appropriation Committee are stricken out, diminished, or increased. The Appropriation Committee, no doubt, exercises a great prestige, but it is the majority in the House that sustains their wisdom or rejects it.

V. The standing Committees are not appointed by Congress at all, but by the Speaker, who at the beginning of each new Congress appoints the standing Committees, who serve during that Congress, or, in other words, for two sessions.

As for their independent action, it should be remembered that the Appropriation Committee has no power whatever to force an Act or insist upon it. It is simply the upper servant of the House, whose duty it is to look well into the estimate made by the Departments, and give a full explanation to the House why such an item should be rejected, reduced, or advanced, and it is for the House to judge how far the Appropriation Committee have acted right.

VI. There can be no legislation in Congress without standing Committees, and the first thing that the elected Speaker does is to appoint the standing Committees.

VII. Certainly. At this very session the estimates as proposed by the Government are being cut down some 18,000,000 or 20,000,000 dols. Of course it remains to be seen whether the service will suffer by it ; but there cannot be the slightest doubt that this revision of Government estimates by the Appropriation Committee first, and finally by the whole members of the House, has the effect of keeping down charges and effecting wholesome reforms.

I have the honour to remain,

Yours very faithfully,

(Signed)   J. S. MOORE.

To T. B. POTTER, Esq., M.P.

H

Reply of Mr. Horace White, *Editor of the " Chicago Tribune."*

Chicago, Illinois, July 13, 1876.

Sir,—In reply to your circular of the 28th ultimo, making certain inquiries respecting the means adopted in America for criticising and controlling the expenditures proposed by the Executive Government, I send the following answers corresponding with the numbers of the several queries proposed :—

I. At the commencement of each regular session of Congress, the Secretary of the Treasury transmits to the House of Representatives a minutely detailed statement of the estimates of appropriations required for each department of the public service for the next ensuing fiscal year. These estimates are prepared by the several departments respectively, and transmitted to the Secretary of the Treasury, by whom they are consolidated and arranged prior to their transmission to the House.

II. Printed copies of the estimates are furnished to all members of the House, and the subject is specially referred to the Committee on Appropriations, who are supposed to pass upon each item separately. When the Committee make their report in the form of an Appropriation Bill, it is the practice of members to discuss the proposed items in full assembly.

III. It is the practice of the legislature to divide the proposed expenditures into the several heads representing the principal departments of the public service. Such divisions of expenditure are not referred for consideration to separate Committees.

IV. All decisions of the Committee of Appropriations are subject to the revision of the House, but not of the Executive Government.

V. No special arrangements are made to secure the independent action of the Committees or the House ; they are supposed to be independent without any special provision for making them so.

VI. Answered by previous observations.

VII. It has been found in experience that the course pursued by the legislative body in the investigation of proposed items of expenditure has had the effect of keeping down the charges recommended by the Government, and of limiting abuses in administration.

After the passage of Appropriation Bills by the House of Representatives they go to the Senate, where the same process is followed both as to Committees and general debate, and final decision.

Balances of Appropriations remaining unexpended at the end of the fiscal year for which they are authorised, are turned back into the Treasury, and cannot be drawn out again without a new Appropriation.

A limited number of Appropriations, including that for interest on the public debt, are " permanent ; " that is, the money required for them can be drawn at any time when needed, irrespective of the annual Appropriations of Congress.

I remain, &c.,

(Signed)   HORACE WHITE.

To T. B. POTTER, Esq., M.P.

Reply of MR. CHARLES NORDHOFF.

918, *Scott Place, Washington, Aug.* 17, 1876.

DEAR SIR,—In reply to yours of the 28th June, I have only now secured time to say :—

I. The Secretary of the Treasury presents, at the beginning of the session of Congress, to the Speaker of the House of Representatives, " Estimates of Appropriations required for the Service of the Fiscal Year ending——." In this book, of which I send you a copy by the present mail, the proposed expenditures are given, as you will perceive, in detail ; together with the actual appropriations in the same detail for the preceding year.

II. The regular practice of the House of Representatives was formerly to separate these heads, and refer each to a distinct Committee. Thus the Committee on Foreign Affairs would scrutinise the estimates for Foreign Intercourse; the Committee on Naval Affairs those for the Navy, &c. But within the last ten years a custom has grown up, under which the Appropriation Committee makes the scrutiny of the whole book of estimates, or at least of parts as it chooses. At the session just closed this Committee undertook the whole estimates, except what is known as the River and Harbour Bill, which comes in the book I send you under Public Works. Members of long experience believe that the recent practice is not judicious. It imposes undue burdens on a single committee, which was originally created for a minor and different purpose. I have no doubt myself that the former plan was the best.

III. The Committee, having perfected its scrutiny of one head, say of the Foreign Service, reports a Bill to the House, which thereupon considers it in committee of the whole, where it may be amended, accepted, or re-committed with instructions. (This answers also No. I V.)

V. The Committees are appointed by the Speaker of the House, who is himself elected by the House, and, of course, represents the opinions of the majority of the House. Committees consist of seven, nine, or eleven members, the majority consisting of members of the majority of the House. It is usual for the chairman of a Committee to consult with the head of the department or bureau whose estimates he has under consideration, and to ask for and receive further information if he needs it.

VI. The expenditures are for the most part made under laws regularly enacted, which prescribe the pay of the officers, from the highest to the lowest; and these laws are seldom changed; and it is held that they should not be changed in an Appropriation Bill, but by separate enactment. The House, however, prescribes the number of persons who may be appointed or retained in the different classes; as for instance, it would enact a special law to change the wages of seamen or the salaries of naval officers, but in the naval Appropriation Bill it would prescribe the number of seamen to be carried on the rolls, &c. The Appropriation Bills, when passed by the House, are sent to the Senate, where also they are examined by appropriate Committees, reported to the Senate, debated, and if the Senate disagrees on any Bill of this (or any other) kind, a Committee of Conference is demanded, consisting usually of three of each body, where the details in dispute are re-considered, and an agreement arrived at, which then is reported to each House, and adopted; or there may be still further disagreement by one House, the Conference report not being necessarily final.

VII. To your seventh question I answer yes—*measurably*, charges are kept down and abuses limited; and I might say even to a very great extent; because the minority is vigilant, and reports to the country any abuses it may discover; and the majority is then constantly on the defensive, and forced to guard against extravagance and abuse. The party now in power, and which has held power since 1861, has gradually reformed and reduced the public expenditure since the close of the war. At the present session the opposition had a predominance in the House of Representatives, and made further and important reductions, as you will have seen in our newspapers; some of these being opposed by the Senate, which remained Republican, or favourable to the Administration.

Our different State legislatures control their expenditures in various ways; but on the same general theory and system above described. With us the most serious problem in relation to Government or public expenditure is found in the large cities, almost all of which have through years of careless and ignorant mismanagement become seriously involved in debt, and yet have not, in most cases, secured efficient government, or that degree of comfort and security which the inhabitants ought to get.

Yours very truly,

(Signed)   CHARLES NORDHOFF.

To THOS. BAYLEY POTTER, Esq.,
  Cobden Club.

Reply of Mr. JOHN T. HOFFMAN, *late Governor of the State of New York.*

New York, *July* 20*th*, 1876.

SIR,—In reply to the questions asked in the enclosed printed circular letter, I have to say :—

-I. " The Government" in the United States, through the Secretary of the Treasury, who is one of the President's Cabinet, does, once in each year, submit to Congress, which is the Legislature of the country, a statement of the purposed items of expenditure for the current year.

II. All proposed items of expenditure, whether suggested by the Secretary of the Treasury or otherwise, are first considered in and acted upon by the " Committee of Ways and Means" (so called) of the House of Representatives (the Lower House of Congress), and the Committee report thereon to the House.   This report is discussed in full assembly of the House, which approves or modifies the same, as the case may be.   Each item of proposed expenditure to which any objection is made or in which any change is suggested is acted upon separately.

When the Lower House has concluded its consideration of the matter, and passed the Bill, it goes to the Senate (which is the Upper House), where it is considered and discussed both in the " Committee on Finance," so called, and in full Assembly of the Senate.

If the Bill, as passed by the House of Representatives, is approved by the Senate without amendment (which is seldom if ever the case), it is at once sent to the President for his approval.   He has ten days in which to approve it, or to return it with a statement of his objections.   This last is called a " veto."

If the House Bill is amended in the Senate in any way, it is sent back to the Lower House for concurrence in the amendments.   If the Lower House concurs, the Bill is engrossed, and sent to the President, who may approve or veto as in the other case.   If the House does not concur in the Senate amendments, Committees of conference of the two Houses are appointed. When they come to an agreement, they report their action to the two Houses respectively, and this Report is generally agreed to. The engrossed Bill is then sent to the President, who may approve or veto. The almost, if not quite, universal practice is to approve. If he should return the Bill with his objections, it cannot become a law unless his veto is overruled by a vote of two-thirds of all the members of each House present when the vote is taken.

III. It is the practice to divide the proposed expenditures into several heads, representing the principal departments of the public service, but these divisions are not referred to separate Committees. There are separate Committees, to which matters relating to the several departments are referred, but all propositions involving the appropriation and expenditure of money are referred, as already stated, to the Committee of Ways and Means. (Recently a new Committee called the Committee on Appropriations has been created, which fixes the amounts of Appropriations, formerly done by a sub-committee of the Ways and Means).

The secretary of the Treasury is at liberty to make any explanations to this Committee, but he has no seat in either House, and can take no part in the discussion in full Assembly.

IV. The Committee's decision, as already stated, is subject to the revision of the legislative branch of the Government. The President, who represents what, I suppose, is in England commonly called " the Government," cannot " revise." He can only veto the Bill, stating his reasons. If the Bill is not passed, as already explained, on his veto, a new Bill must be passed, modified so as to meet the President's objections. This must also pass through the Committee, and be subject to discussion in full Assembly, as in the first instance.

V. The Committee of Ways and Means is selected from among the members of the House by the presiding officer, who is called the Speaker. No arrangements are deemed necessary to secure their independent action, as they are in no way dependent upon or answerable to the executive branch of the Government. The Senate usually appoints its own Committees by vote, the members of the Committees being first agreed upon in a caucus or consultation of a majority of the senators, representing for the time being the dominant political party of the country.

VI. How the legislature may check or control the proposals of the Government with respect to national expenditure already appears.

What I have said relates especially to the general Appropriation Bills, covering the estimates of the Secretary of the Treasury. The remarks are applicable as well, however, to special laws which are often passed, founded upon some particular expenditure. These are not necessarily suggested by the Government. They often originate in Congress.

VII. It is not easy to answer the seventh question satisfactorily, our experience has been so varied. The executive and the legislature are checks upon one another. My own impression is that the tendency of the Legislature has been as often to exceed as it has been to diminish the proposed expenditure of "the Government."

At the present time, however, a determined effort is being made in the Lower House, which is in political opposition to the President and to the Senate, to cut down very materially the proposed expenditure.

It may not be out of place for me to add a few words in regard to the expenditure of the State of New York, which is in population the chief of the United States, its population being about four and a half millions. Each State in the Union regulates its own expenditure for State and local purposes, under its own constitution and laws.

The chief executive officer of New York is called "the Governor;" he is elected by the people for a term of three years. The chief financial officer is called "the Comptroller;" he is also elected by the people. The legislature is composed of a Senate and Assembly—the first composed of 32, and the last of 128 members, all elected by the people, the Senators from Senate districts, the Assembly from Assembly districts.

The Comptroller submits to the Legislature annually an estimate of the proposed expenditure of the several departments of the State government, including the support of public schools, interest upon the public debt, and such sums as may be necessary to pay any maturing principal thereof. All these estimates are first considered by the Committee of Ways and Means of the Assembly, and discussed in full session of the House, and afterwards by the Finance Committee of the Senate, and in full session of the Senate. If necessary, Conference Committees are appointed ; here also all the committees are independent of the executive department of the Government.

On the passage of a Bill appropriating money, the question is taken by yeas and nays, and three-fifths of all the members elected to either House are necessary to constitute a quorum.

The Bill, when passed, is sent to the Governor for approval. He may oppose it or return it with his objections, which are entered on the journal, and which can only be over-ruled by a vote of two-thirds of *all the members elected to each House.*

When I was Governor of New York I suggested an amendment to the Constitution, which would enable the Governor to veto any objectionable items in an Appropriation Bill, and approve the others, so that the Bill as passed would stand, except as to the items not approved. The legislature may, of course, over-rule the veto, as in other cases. This amendment has been adopted, and will, without doubt, produce good results. Whatever may have been the experience elsewhere, I do not hesitate to say that in the State of New York the tendency of the legislature has been to increase rather than diminish the expenditure proposed by the executive department.

Although I have dated this letter " New York," I have written it at a place of summer resort, away from books and papers, and with the mercury ranging above 90° (Fahrenheit) in the shade. I trust, however, you will be able to read it. I take pleasure also in sending you a copy of an " address " which I made in New York last winter, on questions connected with our Government.

Very respectfully yours,

John T. Hoffman.

Thomas Bayley Potter, Esq.,
   Hon. Sec. Cobden Club.

Reply of Mr. A. Pratt.

74, Sargeant Street, Springfield,
Mass., Aug. 9th, 1876.

Dear Sir,—I have had the honour to receive the circular issued by the Cobden Club asking certain questions " with reference to the means adopted in America for criticising and controlling the expenditure proposed by the executive Government."

I am not familiar with the practice of other States than Massachusetts, in relation to the questions asked by you, but have no doubt it is substantially the same in all of them.   In Massachusetts all matters relating to the expenditure of money that come before the legislature are referred to a Committee on Finance.   This Committee, during the first week of each session of the legislature, prepares the Appropriation Bills for the year ; these Bills are for the maintenance of the Government, and set apart certain sums, mostly fixed by statute, for the expenses of the Executive, the Judicial, the Legislative, the Charitable, the Reformatory, and the Agricultural Departments ; for the expenses of the offices of the Secretary of State, the Treasurer, the Auditor, the Attorney-General, and of the military service, and the various Commissioners (Savings Banks, Insurances, &c.).   When these Bills are ready the Committee reports them to the Legislature.   Being based on existing laws, they are carefully scrutinised in open session of the Legislature to secure their strict conformity to the laws, and are passed without debate.

The above Bills you will perceive cover the ordinary expenses of the State. The Committee on county estimates examines the reports from the several boards of county officers asking for the necessary Appropriations to defray county expense, and recommends that such amounts be granted by the legislature as the wants of the several counties seem to require. The legislature discusses, amends, increases, or diminishes the amounts at its pleasure. In cases of unusual or extraordinary expenditures (such as building new prisons or the Hoozac tunnel), the Committee having the matter in charge recommend to the legislature the appropriation of certain sums for the purpose.

Their recommendations are open to debate, amendment, and rejection, but are always referred to the Committee on Finances, to ascertain their bearing upon the condition of the Treasury, or of existing laws, before their passage.

The foregoing, I think, covers all your questions except the last. Whether the course adopted by the legislature, as stated above, is the best to secure an economical administration of the affairs of State, or of limiting abuses in such administration is a question. The experience of many years seems to indicate that the practice has been and is reasonably satisfactory.

I am yours, very faithfully,

EDWIN A. PRATT.

To T. B. POTTER, Esq., M.P.

NO. I.

Article of the London "Economist" of 12th August, 1876.

THE COBDEN CLUB AND THE PUBLIC EXPEN-DITURE OF FOREIGN COUNTRIES.

In view of the continuous and of late increasingly rapid growth of National Expenditure, it is not surprising to find that those whose efforts to keep that expenditure within more moderate dimensions have proved unavailing, are now entertaining and expressing doubts as to the efficiency of the control which Parliament is able to exercise over the Budgets, and a desire to see other and more effective checks imposed upon what they regard as the profusion and extravagance of the Government. Impelled by such motives, and acting at the suggestion of Mr. Bright, the Committee of the Cobden Club have drawn up and forwarded to many of their foreign members a series of questions regarding the means adopted in other countries for criticising and controlling the expenditure proposed by the Executive Governments. The points upon which information is asked are the following :—

1. Does the Government at the commencement, or at any other stated period of the session of the Legislature, announce in detail the proposed items of expenditure for the current year? or in what other manner are such proposals of expenditure brought under the review of the Legislature?

2. Is it the practice of the members of the Legislature to discuss the proposed items of expenditure in full assembly, or are means taken, by the appointment of Committees of the Legislature, or otherwise, to investigate the proposed items of expenditure?   •

3. Is it the practice of the Legislature to divide the proposed expenditure into the several heads representing the principal departments of the public service? and are such divisions of expenditure referred for consideration to separate Committees?

4. If such examination of the details of the proposed expenditure takes place by Committees appointed for such purpose, are the decisions of such Committees in regard to any reduction of expenditure subject to the revision of the Government or of the Assembly?

5. If such Committees are appointed by the Legislative body, what arrangements are made to secure their independent action?

6. In the absence of the appointment of Committees, are any other special means adopted by the Legislature to check or control the proposals of the Government with respect to the national expenditure?

7. Has it been found in experience that the course pursued by the Legislative body in the investigation of proposed items of expenditure, either in the military, naval, or civil services, has had the effect of keeping down the charges recommended by the Government, or of limiting abuses in administration.

To these questions a number of replies have already been received, amongst the most important of them being a very lucid exposition by M. Léon Say, the French Minister of Finance, of the system of control adopted in his country. M. Say's statement is a lengthy one, but the following are its principal points.

In France, the Budget is introduced a year in advance, the estimates for the year 1877, for example, having been laid upon the table of the Chamber of Deputies about the middle of March last. The *Projet de Budget*, as it is called, makes up a very bulky yellow book, a copy of which is placed in the hands of every member of the Chamber. So minutely does it enter into details, that in the volume for the ensuing year—we are told by another correspondent of the Club—no less than 1,220 pages are taken up by the enumeration of the various items of income and expenditure, the latter being given separately for each of the public departments. It further comprises a commentary by the Minister of Finance upon the Budget of the year; schedules of all taxes, rates, and duties to be levied, and the amounts they are expected to realise; a comparison of these figures with those of the previous year; and a statement of all extraordinary income and expenditure. Like all other Bills submitted to the Assembly, the Budget is in the first place referred to the eleven bureaux, or committees, into which that body is each month divided by lot. These committees, however, do not enter into any discussion regarding it, but merely nominate three of their number to a special Budget Committee, which thus consists of thirty-three members, and which is commissioned to inquire into and to report upon the Government proposals. The first step taken by this Budget Committee is to divide itself into as many sub-committees as there are public departments. Each sub-committee takes up the accounts of one department, which it goes over and votes upon, clause by clause, and when it considers it necessary to have further information regarding any of the items in the accounts, it has power to call before it and to examine either the Minister at the head of that department, or any of the officials connected with it. The sub-committee having finished their investigations report to the full Budget Committee, and that in its turn draws up a report upon the whole Budget, which is laid upon the table of the Chamber, and printed and distributed amongst the members. The decisions of the Budget Committee, however, although arrived at after such mature deliberations, are binding upon no one. They are merely presented as recommendations to the Assembly, which after receiving them, proceeds to the public discussion upon the estimates, and in the course of that discussion "the Government may succeed in obtaining in full Assembly credits which the Budget Committee has proposed to suppress;" or on the other hand, the Chamber may decide against an expenditure recommended by the Committee. The Budget, as finally adopted by the Chamber of Deputies, is remitted to the Senate, where it is subjected to a similar course of investigation, save that the Budget Committee of the Senate is composed of only eighteen members. To the question as to whether or not this system has proved effectual in keeping down expenses, M. Say replies:—"The system adopted in France subjects the Government to a very effective control so far as regards the necessity and utility of the credits asked for. Unfortunately, however, members of Parliament in France are not, as in England, debarred from taking the initiative in proposing, either by motions or amendments, new items of expenditure or augmentations of the votes. The equilibrium proposed by the Government is thus in danger of being destroyed by those very persons whose proper duty it ought to be to act as a check upon the public departments in the matter of expenditure, instead of encouraging them to augment their Budgets."

The same objection to the French system is urged by Count Franqueville, who writes :—" It must be noticed that the general principle of the English Constitution—that no money may be voted, and no grants increased, without a special recommendation from the Government—is not admitted by the French law, so that every member has the right to propose, and the Assembly has the right to vote, any sum it likes without limitation." And the opinion of the Count is that—" It has been found that the course pursued by the Assembly has not the effect of keeping down the charges recommended by the Government, or limiting the abuses of the Administration."

As regards the course of procedure adopted in Belgium, very full and interesting details are furnished by M. Adolphe Lehardy de Beaulieu. There, the law demands that the Budget shall be laid upon the table of the Chamber of Representatives not later than the 1st of March, and that it shall set forth every item, both of the ordinary and extra· ordinary income and expenditure, showing separately and in detail the amounts required by each of the public departments. In the first instance, the Budget proposals are referred to the six Sections into which the Chamber is divided, by ballot, at the beginning of every month. Each of these Sections has power to suggest amendments, to propose the rejection of certain items, or to move the addition of new votes. A report of its proceedings having been drawn up and adopted, each Section elects one of its number to carry that report to, and support it in, what is called the Central Section, which is composed of the six delegates, and is presided over by the President or the Vice-President of the Chamber. Like the French Budget Committee, this Central Section has authority to order the attendance of any of the Ministers, or their officials. It first of all makes itself acquainted with the amendments proposed by the six Sections, then proceeds to discuss, item by item, the Budget proposals; and thereafter decides which, if any, of the Sectional amendments ought to be supported. It has also the initiative in proposing new amendments, and its final decisions are embodied in a report which is presented to the Chamber of Representatives, and distributed amongst the members. Then follows the public discussion in the Chamber of Representatives, in the course of which the amendments proposed by the Central Section are adjudicated upon, and finally adopted or rejected either in whole or in part. At the conclusion of the debate every member of the House is called upon by name to record his vote either for or against the Budget as finally arranged, any member who may decline to vote being required to state the reason for so doing. The Budget is then carried by message to the Senate, which has equal power with the Chamber of Representatives to reject or amend any of its propositions, but which cannot, like the latter body, take the initiative in proposing new expenses or sources of revenue. The Senate also refers the Bill to several Special Committees, but the proceedings are for the most part formal, and for the past fourteen sessions the Upper Chamber has suggested no alterations in the proposals submitted to it.

In theory, then, a very perfect supervision of the Government has been established. When, however, M. de Beaulieu comes to speak of the practical working of the system, he has to confess that, so far as the keeping down of expenses is concerned, it has signally failed. The expenditure in 1835 was 87,000,000 fr., while in 1875 it had risen to 256,000,000 fr., and is still rapidly increasing. But M. de Beaulieu is of opinion that the system has failed because, owing to the peculiar political condition of Belgium, it has never received a fair trial. So grossly unequal and unfair is the electoral division of Belgium, and so great the electoral corruption, that a minority of electors have for years been able to return a very strong Parliamentary majority. That minority, too, has an interest opposed to retrenchment. Out of the 115,000 voters entered in the electoral lists, only about 90,000 or 100,000 record their votes, and of these from 40,000 to 50,000 are public servants who have a direct interest in maintaining or increasing the expenditure of the various departments. As matters now stand, it is in the hands of these public servants and of the Roman Catholics —who, as a rule, vote blindly according to the dictation of their priests—that the representation of the country mainly rests, and the representatives of both these sections support the Government in resisting in the House of Representatives any retrenchments that may be recommended by the central section. With equality of representation and purity of election the present system, M. de Beaulieu thinks, might work well.

The course of procedure adopted in Holland, as set forth by Prof. Vissering, is almost identical with that above described. The Budget, which must be complete, detailed, and distinct for each department, is first submitted to the five sections of the Chamber ; each of these sections after discussing the measures, nominates a Reporter (*rapporteur*), and the five Reporters consider the amendments of the various sections, and adopt those which they deem worthy of support. Their decisions are communicated to the Minister in charge of the department interested, who replies, either maintaining his original proposals or modifying them as suggested, and this correspondence is laid before Parliament. The Second Chamber, which is free to deal as it sees fit with the recommendations of the Reporters, and also of its own motion to modify in any way the proposals of the Government, then . discusses the Budget, and finally the measure, when it leaves the Second Chamber, passes to the First Chamber of the States-General, where it is examined and discussed in the same manner. In the Upper House, however, no amendment can be proposed. Prof. Vissering is of opinion that, " Beyond any doubt these regulations have the effect of not only limiting but of preventing all abuses in our financial administration." They have not, it

I

is true, prevented a large increase of yearly expenditure in the last twenty-five years, but that increase " has taken place with the full assent of the States-General, sometimes even on their instigation. And the larger expenses are sufficiently met by constantly growing receipts from different sources, without increasing the burdens of the nation by new taxes."

A similar assertion, however, may be made regarding the expenditure of this country, the growth of which is in some quarters exciting so much dissatisfaction. And it may be doubted whether under any system the expenditure of a country which is increasing in population and in wealth can be prevented from augmenting. This much at any rate is certain—that it is impossible for us to lay down any hard and fast line, whether at £70,000,000 or £80,000,000, and to assert with reason that on the one side of that lies economy and on the other extravagance. The expenditure must be judged of not by its amount only, but also by its objects. There is always, however, on the part of those who are spending other people's money a tendency to go beyond the limits of exact economy, and it would undoubtedly be a great national gain if some method could be devised by which extravagance would be thoroughly repressed, and the national expenditure subjected to so strict a scrutiny that no increase of public burdens would be permitted until its necessity or expediency had been fully demonstrated. In attempting something in that direction, the Cobden Club is doing useful work ; and if the question of the reform of our existing system is mooted, its intelligent discussion may be greatly facilitated by the knowledge of the systems in operation elsewhere, which is now being obtained.

NO. II.

Article from the London "Economist" of 19th August, 1876.

THE CONTROL OF EXPENDITURE IN FOREIGN COUNTRIES.

IN a recent issue we briefly summarised a few of the communications that had been received by the Cobden Club in response to their circular soliciting from the foreign members of the Club information "with reference to the means adopted in other countries for criticising and controlling the expenditure proposed by the Executive Government." Since then we have had communicated to us, amongst others, a number of replies from correspondents in the United States of America, giving very full details of the mode of procedure there adopted in introducing and discussing the Budget Estimates. From these we gather that prior to the commencement of each Session the various departments of the Federal Government are required to draw up and submit to the Secretary of the Treasury detailed estimates of their expenditure for the next fiscal year, commencing on the 1st of July. These are called Bills of Appropriations, and combined they form the Estimates of Appropriation, which the Secretary of the Treasury, who is not a member of either House of Congress, transmits by letter to the Speaker of the House of Representatives, generally within the first week of the Session. By the Speaker they are referred to a standing Committee, called the Committee on Appropriations, which, like all the other Committees of the House, is nominated by the Speaker himself, and not appointed by the House. Incidentally, the estimates come under the cognisance of the various Committees—such as as those on foreign affairs,

military affairs, &c.—which permanently exercise a supervision over the several executive departments of the Government; but it rests with the Committee of Appropriations to
institute a detailed investigation into, and to report upon, the
financial proposals of the Treasury. To that end they confer
with the heads of the Government departments, and summon
before them and examine such witnesses as they deem expedient; and as the result of their inquiries they may suggest the
rejection, reduction, or augmentation of any of the proposed
votes. They have also the power, which is very frequently exercised, of proposing new items of expenditure, but they cannot
in any way enforce the adoption of their recommendations.
These they merely report to the House of Representatives,
which then proceeds to the public discussion of the estimates,
and finally decides which, if any, of the proposed modifications
or additions shall be authorised. The whole Bill, as revised
and amended, is then voted upon, and if approved of is
remitted to the Senate. There it passes through a similar
ordeal. First of all it is referred to the Committee of
Finance, whose powers are identical with those of the Committee on Appropriations in the other House; from the
Committee it goes back to the Senate, which has equal
authority with the Lower House to alter or extend its provisions. In the Senate the Bill is publicly discussed, and if,
as is most commonly the case, in the course of that discussion
modifications are introduced, the Bill must be sent back to
the House of Representatives for concurrence in the amendments. Should that concurrence be obtained the Bill is at
once engrossed; if not, each House appoints a Committee
of Conference, and these two Committees, after consulting
together, draw up a joint Report, to which both Chambers
almost invariably agree. The Bill when thus arranged is
submitted to the President, who may either approve of or
veto it. In the latter case the Bill would be sent back to
Congress, along with a statement of the President's reasons
for refusing to sign it, and it would then be necessary either
to pass it over the veto by a two-thirds majority in each
House, or to originate a new Bill, giving effect to the views

of the President. As yet, however, it has been the invariable practice for the President to approve of the estimates which have been accepted by both Houses of Congress.

Thus far, then, it would seem that very efficient provision has been made for Parliamentary control over the expenditure, but custom appears to have sanctioned an infraction of the law by which that control is to a large extent vitiated. "It is forbidden by law," says a joint report by Mr. D. A. Wells and Mr. L. F. S. Foster—who from 1865 to 1869 acted as Vice-President of the States—"for any department to incur any expenditure other than those which are authorised by law, but these provisions are almost always, in greater or less degree, evaded, and 'deficiency bills' form a part almost invariably of the Appropriation Acts of each Session."

Obviously, this opens the door to many abuses, and to some extent explains the difference of opinion that we find existing amongst the correspondents when they come to deal with the question as to whether or not "the course pursued by the legislative body has had the effect of keeping down the charges recommended by the Government, or of limiting abuses in administration." To that Mr. Moore, of New York, answers with a very decided affirmative, and points out that in the present Session the estimates "are being cut down by some 18,000,000 dols. to 20,000,000 dols." though, he adds, "of course it remains to be seen whether the service will suffer by it." Mr. Hoffman, at one time Governor of New York, speaks with more hesitation. "My own opinion is," he says, "that the tendency of the Legislature has been as often to exceed as to diminish the proposed expenditure of the Government." But he adds, "at the present time, however, a determined effort is being made in the Lower House, which is in political opposition to the President and to the Senate, to cut down very materially the proposed expenditure."

That attempt we now know has been successful, and instead of a reduction of 20,000,000 dols., as Mr. Moore anticipated, the Appropriations for the current year show a

decrease of 29,584,000 dols., as compared with those of
1875. But the minority of the Lower House are freely
expressing their belief that this is only a political stratagem.
The Democrats, they say, desire to appear as the advocates
of retrenchment, and knowing that they can fall back upon
the expedient of "deficiency bills," they have purposely
omitted from the votes several necessary items of expenditure. However that may be, it is the opinion of Mr. Foster
and Mr. Wells, to whose report we have already alluded,
that although the present system of control, if properly
administered, would certainly act as a check upon extravagance, it has yet failed effectively to do so. "The
tendency," they say, "of every department of the Government of the United States, the two Houses of Congress
not excepted, is to continually increase expenditure, and
this increase since 1861 has been very great." Investigations by Congress and discussions by the public have a
counter tendency to repress expenditure and promote
economy, but increasing expenditure is the crying evil at
present in every department of Government in the United
States—State as well as Federal.

In no country does the Budget receive more attention
than in Denmark. Its consideration, in fact, is the chief
business of the Danish Parliament, and the Financial
Committee to which it is referred, has been designated
"the most influential body in the realm."

The course of procedure in regard to the estimates, as set
forth by Count Sponneck and Mr. R. C. Frederiksen, so
closely resembles that adopted in Belgium, to which reference has already been made, that it need now be only very
briefly referred to. At the very beginning of the Session,
the estimates which are given in the most minute detail, are
laid upon the table of the "Folkething" or Lower House.
There is then what may be called a first reading, when
members discuss the general features of the Budget, and at
the close of the debate appoint a Financial Committee of
fifteen members to institute detailed investigations into its
items. That Committee splits itself up into sections, each

section taking the accounts of one department, and when
necessary entering into a written correspondence regarding
them with the officials. The sections report to the Finance
Committee, which after further correspondence with the
heads of the Government department, draws up a report
upon the whole Budget, which is distributed amongst the
members of the Folkething. By them it is discussed in
public assembly, and the Bill as altered or extended in its
provisions, is finally read and voted on a third time, and
then sent to the Landsthing or Upper Chamber. It has
there also to pass through three readings, and in the event
of the two Chambers differing—which is not improbable, as
the Government has a predominating influence in the Upper
House, and there obtains credits which have been denied
by the Folkething—a joint committee of the two Chambers
is formed to bring about a settlement of the points in
dispute. Count Sponneck is of opinion that this course
"has, in experience, proved most efficacious, and sometimes
rather too efficacious to keep down the charges recommended by the Government," and that "the effect of
limiting abuses in administration has been very salutary."
In this view Mr. Frederiksen concurs, and in the course of
an interesting summary of the political condition of Denmark, he throws out the suggestion that the extremely
"demagogical" constitution of the Folkething has a great
deal to do with the economical administration of the
country. An almost universal suffrage throws the Parliamentary representation pretty much into the hands of the
peasantry, or rather peasant proprietors, several of whom
have seats in the Folkething; and they, as a class, "vote
readily for great expenses to railways and schools for the
people, but they seldom incline to vote for salaries exceeding their own very low estimated incomes." In whichever
of these ways it has been brought about—whether by the
excellence of the system of control, or, as is more probable,
from the character of the electors—it is believed that on a
strict comparison the expenditure of Denmark does not show
the growth which characterises that of neighbouring States.

www.ingramcontent.com/pod-product-compliance
Lightning Source LLC
Chambersburg PA
CBHW021818190326
41518CB00007B/647